ON THE JAPANESE ❖ CLASSICS ❖

Conversations and Appreciations

❖

by Daisaku Ikeda

in association with Makoto Nemoto

❖

translated by Burton Watson

New York · WEATHERHILL · *Tokyo*

This book was originally published under the title *Koten o kataru* (Speaking on the Classics) by Ushio Shuppan-sha Co., Ltd, Tokyo, in 1974.

First English edition, 1979

Published by John Weatherhill, Inc., of New York and Tokyo, with editorial offices at 7–6–13, Roppongi, Minato-ku, Tokyo 106, Japan. Copyright © 1974, 1979 by Daisaku Ikeda; all rights reserved. Printed in Japan.

Library of Congress Cataloging in Publication Data: Ikeda, Daisaku. / On the Japanese classics. / Translation of Koten o kataru. / Includes bibliographical references and index. / 1. Japanese literature—To 1600—History and criticism. / 2. Buddhism in literature. / 3. Ikeda, Daisaku—Interviews. / 4. Authors, Japanese—20th century—Interviews. / I. Nemoto, Makoto, 1906–76, joint author. / II. Title. / PL726.115.13713 / 1979 / 895.6′09 / 78–26624 / ISBN 0–8348–0140–X

❖ ❖ ❖ ❖ ❖ ❖ ❖ ❖ ❖ ❖ ❖ ❖ ❖ ❖ ❖

Contents

❖ ❖ ❖ ❖ ❖ ❖ ❖ ❖ ❖ ❖ ❖ ❖ ❖ ❖ ❖

Part Two: The World of the *Kojiki*

2   Myth and Universality   *49*

3   The *Lotus Sutra* and Japanese Mythology   *72*

Part Three: The World of *The Tale of Genji*

Part Four: The World of the *Konjaku Monogatari*

❖ ❖ ❖ ❖ ❖ ❖ ❖ ❖ ❖ ❖ ❖ ❖ ❖ ❖

Preface

❖ ❖ ❖ ❖ ❖ ❖ ❖ ❖ ❖ ❖ ❖ ❖ ❖ ❖

The classics, those great works of the world's varied literary traditions whose lasting value has earned them that label—what strange things they are! Day after day floods of new books pour out of the printing houses. One of them catches our eye, we pick it up, read it through, and are appropriately impressed. And yet as the days pass by, we find the impression it made upon us fading, until the book no longer remains in our memory.

Not so with the classics. If we have ever felt ourselves drawn to one of them, such as the *Man'yōshū*, the great anthology of ancient Japanese poetry compiled some twelve hundred years ago, the case is quite different. It strikes us as vivid and alive, and that impression, far from fading, remains with us for the rest of our lives. I have often wondered what the secret of such works could be, and in recent years I find myself mulling over the question more and more.

The works that we look upon as classics today were certainly not thought of as such at the time they were first produced. Clearly their authors or compilers did not set out with any such high ambitions of creating a "classic." Yet they did have a kind of love for and attachment to their works. And the person who reads them, because of the power and vividness of the impression such works leave upon him, inevitably finds himself filled with a similar kind of love and attachment. It is this fondness and attachment that persists unchanging over the centuries, regardless of how rapidly and radically the times may change or what alterations may take place in the structure of society. Thus the readers of the present day find themselves moved by such works in the same way as were readers of ancient times. It is this persistent power to move readers and to awaken in them a feeling of lasting attachment, no matter how many centuries may have elapsed, that, I believe, qualifies a work to be looked upon as a classic. Not only literature but all true culture may in a sense be defined as that for which we feel a true and lasting attachment. Without such an attachment, culture can never survive.

What enables a work of literature to inspire such love and attachment in readers is the power and vitality that resides within it, and this vitality is nothing other than a reflection of the vitality of the author himself. When I pause to consider this, I cannot help but wonder at the vividness with which the life and vitality of a single individual can be stored up and conveyed to posterity. More and more in recent years I have come to perceive and appreciate this vitality that resides in the classics, this manifestation of the inestimable worth of the life of the individual that makes it possible for such works to move not only the readers of the author's own era, but countless readers over the centuries that follow, with a force that never diminishes no matter how much time may pass.

On the Japanese Classics, the book that follows, represents a series of discussions held between Professor Makoto Nemoto of Sōka University and myself. They were extremely enjoyable discussions, primarily because, as we talked of our feelings of affection for the various classics of the Japanese literary tradition and examined the qualities that entitle them to be looked upon as such, we were able to discover and appreciate the rare vitality embodied in them, the incalculable richness of the human spirit and its immeasurable power to move one anew. An opportunity to engage in such an undertaking could hardly help but be one of the happiest experiences of a lifetime. It is my hope that, through this book, our readers may be able to share in the experiences we had and to develop a similar affection for the works discussed.

We have dealt with the classics of early Japanese literature, including the *Man'yōshū,* the *Kojiki,* the *Genji monogatari,* and the *Konjaku monogatari.* These are, we believe, works that remain vitally alive today and that tell us not only what the spirit of the Japanese people was in times past but speak to us of the future as well. It is our conviction that a true understanding of the classics is to be gained not through cold and objective analysis alone, but must be accompanied by a feeling of genuine love and affection. Only such an affection will allow one to approach and perceive the living spirit of the author within them. And when one has done so, he will be able, through his reading, to recreate the classics in the present, a source of indescribable delight.

The delight that I myself experienced as I responded to these various classics of the past will be found recorded throughout the book. As only one among countless readers, I perhaps did not always respond with great depth or insight, but the blame for this is not to be imputed to the classics. It lies rather in my own inadequacy as a sounding board. Whatever the failings of my responses, however, I hope the reader will understand that they are those of a simple and ordinary man and one who has approached his task open-mindedly and without pretense or preconception.

DAISAKU IKEDA

❖ ❖ ❖ ❖ ❖ ❖ ❖ ❖ ❖ ❖ ❖ ❖ ❖ ❖ ❖

Translator's Note

❖ ❖ ❖ ❖ ❖ ❖ ❖ ❖ ❖ ❖ ❖ ❖ ❖ ❖ ❖

This book, entitled *Koten o kataru* in Japanese, consists of discussions held between Honorary President Daisaku Ikeda of Sōka Gakkai and Professor Makoto Nemoto. Professor Nemoto, a specialist in Chinese history, was a professor of Waseda University until his retirement. At the time of these discussions, he was a professor of Sōka University. He died in 1976. The discussions, as will be seen, were held at different locations over a considerable period of time.

Highly informal in nature, the conversations center around some of the great works of early Japanese literature, the "classics" of the title. The discussants have not tried to impose any broad framework of interpretation upon the works or to arrive at any systematic conclusions concerning them. Rather they have attempted to define

the particular worth and appeal of each work, to discover
some of the ways in which it is related to the life and
thought of the time, and to suggest what significance it
may hold for our own age. Since most of the works
discussed are available in complete or partial English
translations, English readers may turn directly to the works
themselves to see how their own reactions compare with
those of the discussants.

The principal topics of discussion are four classics of the
Japanese literary tradition—the *Man'yōshū*, the *Kojiki*, the
Genji monogatari, and the *Konjaku monogatari*—though numerous other works are cited or referred to. Since Japanese
readers could be expected to have considerable familiarity
with these works, the discussants did not feel it necessary to
include general descriptions of them in their talks. For the
sake of English readers who may not have such background information, however, I will here give brief expla-
nations of the four works, with data on English translations
where they exist.

MAN'YŌSHŪ

The *Man'yōshū*, or *Collection of Ten Thousand Poems*, the
oldest extant anthology of Japanese poetry, was compiled
in the latter part of the eighth century, perhaps by Ōtomo
no Yakamochi (d. 785), a leading poet and official of the
time. It is divided into twenty *kan*, or chapters, and
contains some forty-five hundred poems written over a
period of about 440 years and representing the work of
several hundred poets. Unlike most later anthologies,
which center about the court, the *Man'yōshū* contains

works from almost every class in society—from emperors, statesmen, and eminent clergy to soldiers, beggars, and prostitutes. Though many of the poems are by men and women living in or near the then capital at Nara, there are also works from the outlying provinces. Two principal poetic forms are employed: the *tanka,* or short poem, consisting of thirty-one syllables arranged in five lines or units according to the syllable pattern 5-7-5-7-7; and the *chōka,* or long poem, a form of undefined length consisting of alternating lines of five and seven syllables and concluding with an extra seven-syllable line. The style of the *Man'yōshū* is for the most part simple and realistic. The sentiments of the writers tend to be expressed sincerely and openly, without the indirection and striving for literary effect so evident in later Japanese poetry. The poems are recorded in a cumbersome writing system that uses Chinese characters at times for their meaning and at other times for their sound alone, making it extremely difficult to read and interpret. Nevertheless, the anthology has exercised a profound influence upon the development of later poetry in Japan and is regarded by many as the highest expression of the Japanese poetic spirit.

The best extensive selection of English translations from the *Man'yōshū* is that prepared by a committee of Japanese and foreign scholars under the auspices of the Nippon Gakujutsu Shinkōkai and published in Tokyo in 1940; this contains one thousand poems. Long out of print, it was reissued by Columbia University Press in 1965 and is available in hard-cover and paperback editions. Most of the *Man'yōshū* translations quoted in the text that follows are taken from this work, as indicated in the notes; the remainder are by the translator.

KOJIKI

The *Kojiki,* or *Record of Ancient Matters,* the oldest extant book in Japan, was compiled at the command of Empress Gemmei and completed in 712. It was written down by a courtier, Ō no Yasumaro (d. 723), on the basis of accounts of the past recited to him by a retainer named Hieda no Are whose sex and exact identity are unknown. It is in three books. The first consists of myths dealing with the creation of heaven and earth and the deities inhabiting them. The second and third sections record the reigns of the successive rulers of Japan from Emperor Jimmu, the legendary founder of the imperial line, down to the reign of Empress Suiko, which ended in 628. Though much of the material dealing with the very early period can hardly be accepted as historically reliable, the numerous myths and legends recorded in the work throw invaluable light on the language, society, and beliefs of ancient Japan. Because of these colorful, earthy, and often moving legends and the many lively songs that are interwoven in them, the book possesses great literary interest and importance. Like the *Man'yōshū,* the *Kojiki* is recorded in Chinese characters used sometimes for their meaning and sometimes for their sound.

A second historical work covering approximately the same period, the *Nihon shoki,* or *Chronicles of Japan,* was compiled in 720 by a group of scholars headed by Imperial Prince Toneri. In thirty chapters, it is written almost entirely in classical Chinese and is strongly influenced by Chinese literary and political ideals. Though far more detailed than the *Kojiki,* it is of less literary interest.

The best English translation of the *Kojiki* is that cited in the text, *Kojiki,* translated by Donald L. Philippi, Princeton University Press and University of Tokyo Press, 1969, available in hard cover and paperback. The *Nihon shoki,* also known as the *Nihongi,* was translated by W. G. Aston under the title *Nihongi: Chronicles of Japan from the Earliest Times to A.D. 697,* published first in 1896 by the Japan Society in two volumes. A single-volume edition appeared in London in 1924, and this was reissued by Charles E. Tuttle Company, Rutland, Vermont and Tokyo, 1972, in paperback form.

GENJI MONOGATARI

The *Genji monogatari,* or *The Tale of Genji,* a fiction work in fifty-four chapters, was written, in part or in whole, in the early part of the eleventh century by a court lady-in-waiting referred to as Murasaki Shikibu or Lady Murasaki. The first forty-one chapters deal with the life and romantic adventures of a handsome and talented prince named Genji; the later chapters, more somber in tone, describe the love affairs of two young men related to Genji. The work, one of the longest in world fiction, is interspersed with numerous poems in tanka form. Though dealing almost exclusively with the court aristocracy, the *Genji* is remarkable for the variety of its incidents and personalities, the subtlety and realism of characterization, and the complexity of its themes. Nothing remotely resembling it in scope and mastery existed in earlier Japanese literature, and no later prose works ever surpassed it. By many it is accounted the greatest work of all Japanese literature.

English readers first became acquainted with this unusual work through the translation by Arthur Waley, published in London over the years 1925 to 1933 and since reprinted in numerous editions. Waley's translation, though somewhat abridged, is a prose masterpiece in its own right and established the *Genji* as one of the major works of fiction in world literature. In 1976 a complete translation by Edward G. Seidensticker, *The Tale of Genji*, was published by Alfred A. Knopf. A Tuttle paperback edition appeared in 1978. Because the Seidensticker translation is more faithful to the wording of the original, it has been used here for quotations from the *Genji*.

Konjaku Monogatari

The *Konjaku monogatari*, or *Tales of Once upon a Time*, which appears to have been compiled around 1120, is a collection of over a thousand tales and anecdotes of a popular nature. The work originally contained thirty-one chapters, but only twenty-eight are extant. Nothing is known concerning the compiler or the exact circumstances of compilation. The stories are classified according to origin into those deriving from India, China, and Japan, respectively. Many are didactic in nature, designed to illustrate and popularize Buddhist doctrines, while others seem intended merely to amuse or astound. The stories deal with persons from all levels of society and provide important data concerning the customs and beliefs of the time.

Though samples from the work have been translated into English, no satisfactory extensive English translation of the *Konjaku* exists at present. Quotations in the text that follows are the work of the translator.

NOTE: Throughout the text, the names of Japanese people living before the Meiji era (1868–1912) are written in traditional order—that is, family name first, personal name second. Post-1868 names are given in Western order—personal name followed by family name.

❖   PART ONE   ❖

The World of the *Man'yōshū*

❖ ❖ ❖ ❖ ❖ ❖ ❖ ❖ ❖ ❖ ❖ ❖ ❖ ❖ ❖

1. The *Man'yōshū* Spirit and the World Today

❖ ❖ ❖ ❖ ❖ ❖ ❖ ❖ ❖ ❖ ❖ ❖ ❖ ❖ ❖

THE SPIRIT OF THE JAPANESE

IKEDA: Some days ago I had to go to Osaka on business, and I was able to take time out from my busy schedule to spend one night in Katano in the suburbs, from where one can see the long line of peaks that make up Mount Ikoma. Sitting in a little summerhouse in the quiet evening, chatting in an easy and relaxed manner with old friends, I almost felt as though I were living back in the ancient times when the poems of the *Man'yōshū* were written.

NEMOTO: Considering how rushed you are most of the time, I imagine you felt the contrast even more strongly.

IKEDA: I happened to have along with me a work by Professor Takashi Inukai, who is so well known for his studies of the *Man'yōshū*. After years of traveling around to the various sites mentioned in the *Man'yōshū*, he sums up his impressions in these words: "In the places associated with the *Man'yōshū,* we find no works of art, no shrines or temples or other man-made things that date from those early times. All we find are mountains and rivers, plants and trees, straits and inlets of the sea, or, nowadays, landscapes that are gradually being changed and effaced by human enterprises." And he adds: "Precisely because there are no visible remains of the men of those times, it would seem to be easier to call back into being in vivid and lively terms their spirit, which still haunts those places." [1]

NEMOTO: I see what he means. Because they are embodied in words rather than material objects, the emotions of the men of ancient times are able to stir our imagination with even greater force and vividness. The poems of the *Man'yōshū* are certainly full of place names. There is probably no other collection of Japanese poetry in which the spirit of the time is so intimately fused with that of the particular place or places depicted in the poems.

IKEDA: Each age in history has its characteristic works of art that stand as symbols of the culture of the age. The Venus de Milo, the Homeric epics, the masterpieces of the Renaissance, the plays of Shakespeare—all represent embodiments in art of the spirit and philosophy of the particular age in which they were produced. In a similar manner, the *Man'yōshū* reflects the hearts and minds of the Japanese of ancient times, their sense of life. And at the same time it is a work that has the power to profoundly move even those of us living today and to inspire us with a feeling of nostalgia for the past.

NEMOTO: Would you say that man as he is depicted in the *Man'yōshū* poems is wholly different from man as we know him today? Or would you say that the poems give expression to a kind of fundamental and unchanging conception of human nature?

IKEDA: Poetry, it has always seemed to me, is a means of giving expression to the subtlest movements of the heart and mind. The fact that we today can respond to the poems of the *Man'yōshū* is proof that they embody truly Japanese sentiments—or perhaps I should say truly human sentiments—of a kind that are unchanging and that transcend the barriers of time and place.

And yet, on the other hand, when we compare ourselves with the men and women of *Man'yōshū* times, we today seem to have lost so much. Our daily lives are so busy that we do not even have the leisure to appreciate the scenes of nature around us. We no longer have the time to think or feel. We are rushed and pressed in everything we do. One of the reasons why we have this keen sense of nostalgia and longing when we read the works of the *Man'yōshū* is that they show us just what the mind and heart of modern man have become. They make us aware of how deep and manifold have been the losses we have suffered.

NEMOTO: I agree with you that poetry is something that gives expression to the innermost feelings of mankind. As the Chinese put it long ago: "Poetry expresses the heart's wishes." That is, if one is to give honest expression to the thoughts and emotions that well up within him, he is almost bound to cast them in the form of poetry. We may find examples of such works in the *Book of Odes,* the great classic of ancient Chinese poetry that was traditionally believed to have been compiled by Confucius. Later Confucian scholars tended to give the poems of the *Book of Odes* a philosophical and moralistic interpretation. But originally they were intended to convey in words, I believe, the fundamental emotions of mankind.

In the same way, as you have said, the *Man'yōshū* gives expression to the fundamental Japanese spirit. As a people, I believe the Japanese can perhaps best be characterized by the term "forthright." Or, to put it another way, they have—or at least at one time had—hearts that were open and direct. Terms such as these were often exploited by the militarists in Japan during the Pacific War and therefore tend to have unpleasant associations, and yet they sum up well the nature of the Japanese people. As you say, however, this spirit of openness and directness that once characterized the Japanese people has been sadly distorted and effaced in modern times.

THE CLEAR LIGHT OF THE SPIRIT

IKEDA: The richness of their natural surroundings, the changes of the four seasons—it was these that nourished the poetic feelings of the men of ancient Japan. The outpourings of hearts and minds that are expansive, open, and outgoing are what we find crystallized in the poems of the *Man'yōshū*. This purity of spirit, as it is affected by the varied scenes of nature and events of human life, seems almost spontaneously to take form in poetry. There is a kind of clear, vivid light of the spirit that seems to pour forth from all the 4,516 poems of the anthology, transcending the centuries that have elapsed since their composition and conveying to us directly the breath of life. It could be described as open and direct, as you have pointed out, or perhaps as clear and bright. We can seen it in the lofty and clear tone of the following famous poem by Emperor Tenji (626–71):

> Over the sea's
> Bright bannered clouds
> The setting sunlight plays:
> The moon tonight—
> How clearly it will shine!

NEMOTO: It is a splendid poem, one that makes you feel clean inside. I wonder there are so few modern poems that have the power to move one in the same way. Of course I'm just an amateur myself and have no real understanding of poetry.

IKEDA: But there ought to be poetry that is capable of moving even amateurs, plain ordinary people like you and me. In fact, that is what true poetry should be like. They say that the decline of poetry means the decline of culture as a whole. I am certainly a rank amateur myself and am hardly qualified to make pronouncements on the literary worth of present-day poetry. And yet modern poetry—and in fact modern literature as a whole—seems so often to be unnecessarily difficult to understand and to be wandering off into trivial bypaths and mazes. I am sure there are very good reasons why it is, and has to be, this way. And yet I cannot help feeling that this kind of following of trends does not represent the proper course for literature. It may be no more than the opinion of an outsider, but I believe that the true goal of literature should be to create works that ordinary people as a whole can respond to—not, of course, shallow or vulgar works, but works of a lofty quality.

NEMOTO: I think we might say that words in the present time have become little more than symbols for the transmission of ideas. We live in a world dominated by machines and government controls, one in which human emotions are suppressed or ignored. Words no longer seem to have the sharpness and clarity they once had. Torrents of words pour out of people's mouths, and yet the impression is one of emptiness. In place of communication, we are left with a feeling of dreary isolation and mistrust.

IKEDA: I am sure that the men of the *Man'yōshū* also had their feelings of loneliness and acute self-consciousness. And yet, even in the midst of such loneliness and self-consciousness, they retained a strong subjective sense of their own potentiality for action. If we look at the period in which they lived, we can see that it was by no means an age of idyllic calm and contentment. Actually, as has often been pointed out, the 150 years represented by the poetry of the *Man'yōshū* was a period of rapid and revolutionary change such as had never been known before in Japanese history.

NEMOTO: Though the flowers bloom
With the same hue unchanging,
The lords and ladies
Of the great palace—
How they have changed!

As we can see from this *Man'yōshū* poem by Tanabe no Fuku-maro, it was a period of constant political struggle and change. Prince Naka no Ōe succeeded in overthrowing the powerful Soga family and instituting the Taika Reforms (645), and in time he came to the throne as Emperor Tenji. Then, with his death in 672, the Jinshin Uprising, which was yet another struggle for power, broke out. In 701 the *Taihō ritsuryō* laws were promulgated, establishing a strong central bureaucracy to rule the nation. This was followed by the moving of the capital to Nara, the sending of official envoys to the T'ang court in China, the casting of the Great Buddha of the Tōdai-ji, and the other innovations of Tempyō-era (729–49) culture. And all the while various attempts to seize political power were taking place. In the area of foreign relations as well, Japan was defeated in Korea and lost the territories on the Korean Peninsula that it had once held. In a sense it was the dawning of Japanese culture, but it was also a period of change and transition not unlike the one we are living in today.

PROFOUND LYRICISM AND VIGOROUS DESCRIPTION

IKEDA: As we survey Japan during the period when the poems collected in the *Man'yōshū* were being written, we find it going through the inevitable process of construction, completion, flourishing, and decay of social and cultural forms and institutions, the process described in Buddhist terminology by the terms *jō, jū, e,* and *kū*—formation, persistence, destruction, and return to emptiness. This process of growth is clearly reflected in the evolution of the poetic style of the anthology as a whole.

NEMOTO: It is indeed. The anthology begins with the famous poem by Emperor Yūryaku (418–79), in which he addresses a young woman in the following terms:

> Your basket, with your pretty basket,
> Your trowel, with your little trowel,
> Maiden, picking herbs on this hillside,
> I would ask you: Where is your home?
> Will you not tell me your name?
> Over the spacious land of Yamato
> It is I who reign so wide and far,
> It is I who rule so wide and far.
> Tell me, then,
> Of your home, and your name. [2]

The poem has an air of simplicity and boldness that reflects the rhythm of life in this early period of growth and development. In contrast with this, we find the poems dating from the latter part of the period increasingly overshadowed by a mood of melancholy and weariness.

The latest poem in the *Man'yōshū* that can be accurately dated, and the last one in the anthology, is that composed by Ōtomo no Yakamochi (d. 785) at a banquet on New Year's Day of 759. The previous year the poet had been assigned to the post of governor of Inaba Province and was thus living in obscurity and disfavor far from the capital.

> Even as the snow falls today
> At the commencement of the New Year
> And with the newborn spring,
> Ever thick come, good things! [3]

The poem is a fervent prayer for good fortune in the year to come, and yet it seems, like so much of Yakamochi's poetry, to be tinged with the sadness of a man who realizes that a period of history is drawing to a close. The period that followed, that of the Heian (794–1185), was dominated by aristocratic tastes.

And though its poetic works are rich in feeling, they tend, in contrast with those of the *Man'yōshū* period, toward excessive concern with literary devices and plays on words and often fall into decadence and superficiality.

IKEDA: I am not sure we are justified in labeling them decadent or effete—they represent, after all, a very different and special kind of style. Personally, however, I find that I am not greatly moved by literary works that are dominated by that kind of aristocratic taste. I much prefer the deep lyric feeling, the openness, and the direct, vigorous descriptive powers that one finds in the *Man'yōshū* poems.

As I mentioned earlier, the *Man'yōshū* poets undoubtedly faced their share of sorrows, complications, and impediments. And yet their works display a kind of forceful, unyielding attitude that is willing to confront the circumstances of life directly. They are filled with a stoutness of spirit that is capable of standing up under the severest strain. There is a healthfulness to them that refuses to be frustrated or broken down.

NEMOTO: In that sense, they are wholly removed from the spiritual condition of our present age. When it comes to human freedom, we see the same contrast. In terms of the formal safeguards set up to protect human rights and liberties, there has never been an age that can equal our own. And yet I cannot help wondering if we are, in the true sense of the word, really free.

For example, freedom of speech is guaranteed to us, and yet are we really able to say exactly what we think? I believe not. For one thing, we are limited in actual fact by various social restraints. And at the same time, we seem to have lost the courage to speak out. We are hindered by a kind of excessive self-consciousness that makes us embarrassed to express ourselves directly and openly.

IKEDA: And so we have a tendency to express ourselves in

indirect and roundabout language. And in doing so, we mistakenly think we are achieving greater subtlety and depth.

ALL MEN ARE POETS

NEMOTO: We make the mistake of believing that direct expression is somehow shallow. When we look at the poems of the *Man'yōshū*, we find that they very frequently employ the same words and phrases. We today would be troubled by such repetitiousness and would look around for some other way of saying the same thing. The *Man'yōshū* poets, however, are perfectly content to employ the identical words over and over again. And yet, strangely enough, their poems do not sound mannered. Because the feelings are expressed with such utter naturalness, they strike one all the more forcibly.

IKEDA: And even when the same words are used, they are endowed with a sense of the inner sincerity and repleteness of the person who employs them. Words, when properly chosen, can convey through their sound the very essence of the life and spirit of the user. This can come across very forcefully and directly in short poems such as the thirty-one-syllable tanka used in the *Man'yōshū* and other early anthologies. To cite a rather well-known example, the *Man'yōshū* contains the following anonymous tanka:

> The lords and ladies
> Of the great palace
> Have leisure enough;
> Here they are out together
> Bedecked with plum flowers. [4]

The *Shinkokinshū* (New Collection of Ancient and Modern Poems, compiled in 1205) contains the same poem, but the closing two lines have been changed to read:

They pass this day too
Bedecked with cherry flowers.

Though the words are almost the same, the force and sonority of the language is very different in the two versions.

NEMOTO: One wonders just why there should be this basic difference between the *Man'yōshū* and the poetry of the ages that came after it. Of course, we can point out that in the period following the time of the *Man'yōshū*, poetry came to be looked upon as a kind of elegant pastime and was an indispensable part of the daily social relations among the members of the upper class. Also we see the appearance of a special group in society, made up of members of the aristocracy and learned monks, who prided themselves upon their expert knowledge of literature. But at the same time that critical taste and literary expertise were increasing, poetry itself tended on the contrary to become less and less realistic in content and feeling.

IKEDA: It may sound like a somewhat overly dramatic way to put it, but in a sense I think we can say that the poems of the *Man'yōshū* represent the sparks thrown off by the combustion of the human spirit in early times. The men and women who produced these poems probably had very little consciousness of literary genres and, in most cases, did not give any deep thought to what sort of social function their works might fulfill. They simply found themselves with a kind of rush of feeling that demanded expression. They were possessed by something that welled up from deep within them. Therefore their works, although they may at times be rather naive and artless in expression, have a sense of realness and urgency about them— they are fashioned out of actual flesh and bone.

NEMOTO: In other words, it was not a question of whether the expression was adequate or inadequate. The poems are the product of realities of daily life that could not be denied expression. When we stop to consider it, we realize that, in the end, poetry and all other literature and philosophy as well are not something that exist in isolation from daily life, but within it, within the pursuit of life itself.

The men and women of the *Man'yōshū* had no elaborate system of philosophy, and yet they had their thoughts and meditations that came to them in the course of life. Any person who grapples seriously with the concerns of human life is bound to be more or less of a philosopher. We often say that all men should possess minds that are capable of philosophizing. The *Man'yōshū* offers extraordinary proof that, in the realm of literature, all men are capable of becoming creators—that, in fact, all men are poets.

IKEDA: I agree completely. The words *man'yō* in the title of the anthology have been interpreted in two different ways. Some scholars would take them to mean "ten thousand words," that is, ten thousand poems; others would interpret them to mean "ten thousand ages," that is, poems that will last forever. Nowadays the latter interpretation seems to be preferred. But in view of the contents of the anthology, the former interpretation appears to me to be more appropriate. The true worth and appeal of the anthology lies in the very breadth of its contents, the fact that it does really contain an almost unlimited variety of poems composed by all kinds of men and women, from emperors, empresses, and members of the aristocracy down to common soldiers, farmers, fishermen, and others of the general populace. It demonstrates that all men are capable of being both creators and appreciators of poetry. Poetry is not the possession of any one special class. It does not give expression to any particular ideology, nor, needless to say, is it marked by any division into schools or styles. Rather it represents a mixture and fusion of classes, ideologies, and styles, and from those sources it draws inestimable power.

We are dealing here, of course, with an early and relatively simple stage in the development of society, long before commercialism or the mass production of literature was even dreamed of. Although there were a certain number of poets who were attached to the court in a more or less professional capacity, on the whole it was an age when poetic creation was an act performed gratuitously and without thought of reward. Also, of course, the people of the time did not have their sensitivities dulled by the kind of confused and excessive flood of data with which modern man is confronted. And yet it was a period that produced countless numbers of poets whose works shine with the light of humanity and ring with the voice of living men and women. It is this astonishing discovery that so strongly impresses those of us in the present age.

THE HEARTFELT SONGS OF THE COMMON PEOPLE

NEMOTO: True poetry, I think we may say, is born out of lives that are fully lived. But the lives of the ancient Japanese, we must remember, were far more communal in nature than ours are today, and their poetry was often the product of group activities such as the dances and exchanges of poems, known as *utagaki*, between men and women. Such rounds and community songs and poems cannot be properly appreciated so long as we approach them with our modern concepts of poetry as an expression of the creative spirit of the individual alone.

IKEDA: Whenever I open the *Man'yōshū*, I am reminded of a great range of mountains. It has its lofty peaks, the poets of towering stature such as Kakinomoto no Hitomaro (fl. 680–700), Yamabe no Akahito (d. ?736), Ōtomo no Tabito (665–731), Yamanoe no Okura (?660–?733), or Ōtomo no Yakamochi (718–85). And yet it is not they alone who give form to the range. In addition, there are the several hundred poems by anonymous writers, probably the product of lower officials or members of the common people, that help to lend splendor to the anthology. These anonymous poems, in fact, often rival the finest compositions of the great poets I have mentioned above. These poems by members of the common people living in poverty and obscurity have a kind of earnest and heartfelt quality to them, a determination to express the writer's own awareness of the worth of life, that never fails to impress me. That is why I am particularly attracted to the groups of anonymous poems known as "Azuma uta," or "Eastland Poems," and the "Sakimori no uta," or "Poems of the Frontier Guards."

NEMOTO: The "Eastland Poems" are recorded in the fourteenth chapter of the *Man'yōshū* and were sung at community gatherings, giving expression to the feelings common to the members of the group. They are products of the labors and daily activities of the common people of the eastern provinces and abound in local flavor, simplicity of feeling, and the healthful vigor of the countryside.

IKEDA: They seem to overflow with the spirit of the common people, the kind of spirit that frankly and openly acknowledges beauty where beauty is to be found, but that at the same time is willing to face up to the realities of daily life, whether pleasant or unpleasant. In other words, they are expressions in poetry of the kind of direct apprehension of life that predates the consciousness of art or literature as such. To be sure, they are often stereotyped in expression, but this in a sense simply serves to prove that the "Eastland Poems" represent the accepted formulations of the sentiments and outlook common to the group as a whole.

NEMOTO: Many of the "Eastland Poems" are *sōmon,* or love poems, quite astonishing in their boldness and directness of expression. And yet we find in them none of the leering quality, the morbid sensuality, that so often characterizes the expression of sexual attraction in literature of the advanced countries of today. They can only be called open-minded.

> Like the bundles of hemp of Aso
> in the fields of Kamitsuke
> I held you in my arms
> as we slept, never tiring—
> what am I to do?

As you can see, the poem is very powerful, and yet not in the least offensive.

IKEDA: Again we find many poems that are filled with tender sentiment, such as the following:

> The road to Shinano
> is a new-cut trail—
> you'll be walking on hacked-up
>   stubs, husband.
> Wear your shoes!

The loving concern that the wife feels for her husband on his journey comes across with great freshness.

> In the twilight,
> that day he crossed
> Mount Usuhi,
> my husband—I saw him clearly—
> waved with his sleeve.

> Even now
> so deep is the love I feel,
> deep as the
> involuted plains
> of Tago.

These examples, too, succeed in conveying very subtle emotion without resort to literary artifice.

NEMOTO: It is a pity that the kind of simple, realistic poems of the populace such as are represented by these "Eastland Poems" are so seldom found in the Japanese literary tradition of later times. At the same time, we cannot help but be impressed that poems such as these should have been composed in the provinces far away from the capital, and that they should have been carefully collected and handed down to posterity. It suggests that, although the capital and the countryside may have been very different in many ways, they were linked at this time by common sentiments that transcended such distinctions. It also suggests that the persons who compiled the anthology must have been highly perceptive.

RECORDS OF THE COMMON PEOPLE: THE "POEMS OF THE FRONTIER GUARDS"

IKEDA: It is interesting to note that, though the *Man'yōshū* contains many poems by emperors, empresses, and other members of the ruling class, it also contains poems by common people expressing opposition to the government, particularly to its conscription of men for military duty. Before the Pacific War, it was even suggested in Japan that such poems, because of their antiwar sentiment, should be suppressed or deleted from the anthology entirely.

NEMOTO: It is this aspect that makes the "Poems of the Frontier Guards" of such interest. The frontier referred to is the Dazaifu, the government office on the far western island of Kyushu. The guards were recruited from the eastern provinces and had to pay their own expenses on the journey as far as Naniwa (present-day Osaka). From there they embarked by ship to Kyushu. The journey by land and sea must have been a very long and hard one. In their poems, the men voice their grief at having to part from their wives and loved ones at home, and their longing for their native region. As we read the poems today, we cannot help but be struck by the poignancy of their sorrow.

IKEDA: The feeling of sadness that is conveyed in the simple and rustic language of the guardsmen from the east seems to symbolize the fate of the common people in all ages who must somehow bear up under the burdens placed upon their shoulders by those in authority. Reading them, I feel more strongly than ever that something must be done to relieve the people of this unhappy lot. However, leaving that problem aside for the moment, we should value the poems of the guardsmen very highly, I feel, because they represent the priceless record of ordinary people who not only bore up under their harsh fate but even found the heart to express their deep-felt emotions in poetry. The poems are rare examples of literature that emerged from the most trying circumstances.

NEMOTO: I would like to quote a few of them to demonstrate the points we have been discussing. The first expresses the sorrow of a man who is forced to part from his wife because of his sense of public duty:

> How awesome
> the imperial command bestowed on me—
> from tomorrow
> I sleep mid grasses,
> no more with my wife.

The next is an example of a poem by the parents of a guardsman:

> Not to stay here
> at home in longing
> but rather I wish to be
> the sword you gird on,
> my son, guarding your life!

The third must be by a young man going off to frontier duty:

> Father and mother
> patting my head,
> saying, "Luck go with you!"—
> how hard
> to forget those words.

IKEDA: There are also poems composed by the wives of the guardsmen:

> "Whose husband this time,
> off to frontier duty?"
> How I eye with envy
> that woman who asks,
> not a worry in her head!

The following one is particularly poignant:

> The children
> who cried,
> dragging on my robe—
> I've gone off and left them,
> and they with no mother.

These, one feels, are not so much poems that have been composed as they are spontaneous outcries of the spirit of men and women who are suddenly faced with a bitter destiny. There is no trace about them of empty lamentation, of symbolic or intellectualized figures of speech. They describe the situation simply and concretely, in the manner characteristic of the *Man'yōshū* as a whole, and thereby achieve great forcefulness of appeal.

NEMOTO: There are also, we may note, certain poems that do not fit into the pattern described above, but rather give expression to a sense of selfless devotion to the ruler. The following is an example, a poem that was included in the anthology *Aikoku hyakunin isshu* (One Hundred Poems of One Hundred Patriots) that was compiled during the war:

> From today on,
> never looking back,
> as a strong shield
> for my lord
> I will go forth!

This was said to have been written by a *kachō*, or lower-ranking officer, who was evidently stirred by the desire for fame and worldly advancement.

IKEDA: Quite possibly. It is certainly representative of the psychology of the petty officer. And yet I can hardly believe that this man was entirely unmoved when the time came to take leave of his family. Rather, he seems to be trying to overcome his emotions by encouraging himself with a show of bravado. He was, after all, a man of the common people like the other frontier guards. I cannot help feeling repelled by the mistaken sense of mission with which he sets off on his journey.

THE BUDDHIST OUTLOOK OF YAMANOE NO OKURA

NEMOTO: This will take us into a somewhat different question from the ones we have discussed so far, but I always wonder at the fact that, although Buddhism was in a very flourishing state during the Nara period (646–794), when the *Man'yōshū* was compiled, there seems to be strangely little reflection of Buddhist ideas in the poetry of the anthology. The Nara period saw the building of the Tōdai-ji and numerous other splendid temples, the arrival of considerable numbers of Chinese monks, the casting of the great bronze image of the Buddha for the Tōdai-ji, and a quite unprecedented flowering of Buddhist sculpture, painting, and architecture. And yet Buddhist ways of thought seem to have exerted very little influence in general.

Several reasons occur to me why this should have been so. For one thing, the type of Buddhism introduced to Japan at this time appealed mainly to the aristocracy and may have been confined largely to a group of educated persons who were closely associated with the central government. Also, it is possible that the indigenous religion of the people still retained such vigor and appeal that it was able to assimilate Buddhist forms and ideas until they no longer retained their distinctive form. Certainly the time had not arrived when Buddhism could penetrate very deeply into the religious life of the common people as a whole.

IKEDA: And yet the view of the present world as transient, as a temporary joining together of elements, which is so typical of Buddhist thought, seems to have prevailed among a certain portion of the population. We can see this Buddhist view of the emptiness and vanity of the world reflected in the numerous poems that Ōtomo no Tabito wrote on the occasion of his wife's death. And the following poem, by an anonymous writer, gives evidence of a belief in a land or world after death:

> Living, living on
> in this bustling inn
> of life,
> and not knowing the shape
> of the land I go to next.

The belief in the transitory nature of the world is evident in the following poem by a man who had entered the Buddhist clergy:

> It is a world of sorrow,
> I said,
> and left it—
> what reason would there be
> to return to it now?

All these poems give expression to the kind of pessimistic and negative view of the world that was to become so pronounced in later ages. And among the poems of Ōtomo no Yakamochi, who belongs to the final period represented in the *Man'yōshū*, we find the following introductory note and poem:

> Desiring to pursue the Way of Buddha while
>   lying in his
> sickbed and lamenting the transcience of life.

> Brief is this mortal life—
> Let me go and seek the Way,
> Contemplating the hills and streams undefiled![5]

And yet one feels that the poem expresses less the poet's burning desire to take up the religious life than it does his wish that, embroiled as he was in political struggles, he might find some means of escape from the realities of his present situation.

NEMOTO: Of all the poets in the *Man'yōshū*, Yamanoe no Okura seems to have had the widest contact with the culture of the continent and to have been most influenced by it in his thinking. In 701 he was appointed a member of the official Japanese embassy to the T'ang court in China, and after his return to Japan in 704 his work shows that he had been deeply influenced by Chinese literature and thought. There is also a theory that he was the descendant of an immigrant family from the state of Paekche in Korea. In any event, he differs somewhat in background and outlook from the other poets of the *Man'yōshū*.

IKEDA: The main body of lyric poetry that makes up the *Man'yōshū* is centered about the court and other persons living in the Nara area. This is enriched and augmented, as we have seen, by the "Eastland Poems" and "Poems of the Frontier Guards," works of the common people living in the provinces of eastern Japan. Yamanoe no Okura's poems in turn add a further breadth and depth to the world of the *Man'yōshū*.

It is true that his works are somewhat lacking in the spontaneous lyric outflow that characterizes most of the other poets of the anthology. But in the manner in which he examines and seeks to get at the heart of human suffering, there is something that suggests a man who is in search of religious truth. If we take the point of view that the true Buddhist spirit is not to be found in superficial observations upon the transitory nature of life or expressions of belief in the Pure Land paradise, but is, rather, in an attitude that seeks to confront the harsh realities of human existence, then Yamanoe no Okura in his thinking is perhaps the most genuinely Buddhist of all the *Man'yōshū* poets. In many ways he resembles Shākyamuni, the founder of Buddhism, who, facing the realities of his own time, sought a solution to the basic problems of human suffering represented by birth, old age, sickness, and death.

NEMOTO: Yamanoe no Okura's most important works are those entitled "An Expostulation to a Straying Mind," "Thinking of Children," "An Elegy on the Impermanence of Human Life," and the famous "Dialogue on Poverty." The introductions that he wrote to these poems, particularly that to the poem "Thinking of Children," give explicit expression to Buddhist views. The last poem mentioned reads:

> When I eat melon,
> I remember my children;
> When I eat chestnuts,
> Even more do I recall them.
> Whence did they come to me?
> Before my eyes they will linger,
> And I cannot sleep in peace. [6]

No other poet in the *Man'yōshū* has written so penetratingly on the instinctive love of a parent for his children. And in his "Elegy on the Impermanence of Human Life," he gives a description, unparalleled in its graphic realism, of the manner in which the beauty and happiness of youth give way to the ugliness of old age.

THE RESTORATION OF HUMAN NATURE

IKEDA: At first glance, Yamanoe no Okura's works often seem to express a kind of despair or abhorrence of the human condition, and yet underlying them one senses a deep feeling of love. The grim "Dialogue on Poverty" by no means makes pleasant reading, concluding its long description of hardship and suffering with the words, "Must it be so hopeless — / The way of this world?" And this is followed by a *hanka*, or envoy, that reads:

> Nothing but pain and shame in this world of men,
> But I cannot fly away,
> Wanting the wings of a bird. [7]

The words would seem to convey a feeling of sorrow at the hopelessness of man's plight, but behind them one senses an unbounded love for humankind.

Yamanoe no Okura's poetic world lacks the kind of beauty and serenity of feeling that we find in the works of other *Man'yōshū* poets. When we compare his works with such masterpieces as this by Kakinomoto no Hitomaro:

> O plovers flying over the evening waves
> On the lake of Ōmi,
> When you cry, my heart grows heavy
> With memories of bygone days. [8]

or this by Yamabe no Akahito:

> Oh, the voices of the birds
> That sing so noisily in the treetops
> Of the Kisa Mountain of Yoshino,
> Breaking the silence of the vale! [9]

we wonder that they should ever be found in the same anthology with these other works. And yet the earnestness with which he strives to convey a sense of reality in his poems, even though his subject may be such ills as poverty, sickness, or old age, give them a beautiful and moving quality of their own.

NEMOTO: After the time of Yamanoe no Okura, themes such as poverty and the other darker aspects of life almost entirely dropped out of the Japanese poetic tradition for a period of many centuries. In China, poverty was often made the subject of poetry, one of the most famous examples being the set of seven poems on poverty by the poet T'ao Yüan-ming (365–427). In most cases, however, such poems are rather glorifications of the simple life of poverty, written by men who, fed up with their positions in the bureaucracy, retired from official life and returned to their homes in the countryside. Other well-known poets such as Tu Fu, Li Po, and Po Chü-i also endured periods of exile or wandering and wrote of their hardships.

But to return to the *Man'yōshū*, I wonder if we might not say that it is a work of literature that, while inspiring us with feelings of nostalgia for qualities of life that appear to have become lost in modern times, also suggests the possibilities for recovering the original purity and human nature.

IKEDA: It is a book that I find myself reading over and over. The breadth and magnitude of the world that is revealed in its pages could be discussed almost endlessly, one feels, without really exhausting the subject. Every time I read it, I find myself delighted by new discoveries. As with all great classics of literature, it reveals just how richly and fully it is possible for human beings to live. There is no truer joy than that to be found in reassuring ourselves of that fact and experiencing it vicariously through the written word.

❖   PART TWO   ❖

The World of the *Kojiki*

❖ ❖ ❖ ❖ ❖ ❖ ❖ ❖ ❖ ❖ ❖ ❖ ❖ ❖

2. Myth and Universality

❖ ❖ ❖ ❖ ❖ ❖ ❖ ❖ ❖ ❖ ❖ ❖ ❖ ❖

THE SORROW OF THE HUMAN HEART

IKEDA: The bush clover is very beautiful at this time of the year.

NEMOTO: There certainly is a lot of it here in the grounds of Sōka University. I gather you are very fond of it.

IKEDA: Yes, very fond of it, indeed! Wherever I go, I am always happy if I find bush clover in bloom, and I never fail to admire it. It is a very elegant flower, and at the same time has a certain force of character. There is an almost indescribable charm about those delicate little pink and white blossoms that come out and then scatter over the ground. It is no wonder that in Japan since ancient times it has been regarded as one of the most beautiful of all the autumn flowers.

NEMOTO: The *Man'yōshū* contains a great many poems descriptive of *hagi*, or bush clover.

IKEDA: The bush clover might be said to be the flower of those who care for peace and culture. I believe it was Yamanoe no Okura who listed it first among the so-called seven flowers of autumn:

> The flowers that blow
> In the autumn fields,
> When I count them on my fingers,
> There they are—
> The flowers of seven kinds.
> They are the bush clover,
> The "tail flower," the flowers
> Of the kudzu vine and patrinia,
> The fringed pink, and the agrimony,
> And last the blithe "morning face." [1]

NEMOTO: For Yamanoe no Okura it is an unusually gentle poem. In his time it was the custom to use the flowers of the bush clover and other plants as decorations for the hair. The *Man'yōshū* contains poems that refer to the custom.

IKEDA: *Kazashi* is, I believe, the term used for such ornamental sprays of flowers or leaves in the hair. They might almost be said to symbolize the tenderness and deep feeling of the men and women of ancient times, who saw their own thoughts and emotions reflected even in the flowers that bloomed by the roadside.

The *Kojiki*, the oldest Japanese work of history, also contains a poem referring to the custom, though the decoration in this case does not happen to be the flowers of the bush clover. It is one of the poems composed by the ancient hero Yamato Takeru no Mikoto when he recalled his native region:

> Let those whose life
> Is secure
> Take from the Heguri Mountains
> (Of the rush matting)

Leaves of the great oak
And wear them in their hair
—O my lads!—[2]

It seems to have been a belief in ancient times that one could insure long life by wearing oak leaves in the hair. One may dismiss it as a silly superstition, and yet I sense in it the sorrow and pain of the human heart, of men who have no recourse but to pray constantly for their safety. It is easy enough to dismiss the irrational elements that we encounter in these accounts of legendary times as mere superstitions. And yet, to do so over- looks the richness of the human spirit that is reflected in them.

A CRITICISM OF REACTIONISM

NEMOTO: Nowadays mythology does not seem to enjoy a very good reputation. Unless we examine it with the cold eye of rationalism and pick it apart, we are not considered to be scientific in our approach. I am something of a scholar of history myself, and yet I find it difficult to approve of such an extreme attitude.

IKEDA: I agree. We are men of modern times, and so long as we try to understand texts like the *Kojiki* through the light of reason alone, I suppose we must label as irrational those elements about it that are in fact irrational.

However, there are things within the deeper layers of the human heart and mind, within the vast sea of life itself, that cannot be grasped by reason alone. They are in no sense contrary to reason, but we might say that they belong to a different spiritual order or dimension. And the same, I believe, can be said of myths. They are indications of just how much, or how little, progress the human mind has made.

Myths are in their essence not the products of reason but are born out of imagination and strong emotional forces. As a result, they reflect the experiences common to men in ancient times in their spiritual and material lives.

NEMOTO: Modern man's tendency is to dissect myths in a clinical fashion and, in the process, to reduce them to lifelessness. But such a thoroughly scientific and rational procedure invites a kind of coldness of heart and may even precipitate spiritual crisis.

IKEDA: I agree. This does not mean, however, that I entirely approve of the spiritualist approach. It may become a cloak for the kind of reactionism of which I have always strongly disapproved. We saw this in Japan in the period before the Pacific War, when the myths of ancient Japan that are recorded in works such as the *Kojiki* were treated as though they represented actual historical fact and were accorded the highest reverence. The abuses that arose as a result were very serious, indeed, and have caused many persons to have unpleasant associations with the *Kojiki* and such texts. I feel that I myself have finally reached the point where I no longer react in that way. But I still remember that the prewar textbooks for elementary school children began their treatment of Japanese history with accounts of Amaterasu Ōmikami, the sun goddess, and she was held up as the eternal and unchanging foundress and protector of the "Great Japanese Empire."

NEMOTO: Yes, in the period before the war the accounts of ancient times recorded in the *Kojiki* and the *Nihon shoki* were taught just as though they were proven historical fact. There was even a national holiday declared—*Kigensetsu* or the Anniversary of Emperor Jimmu's Accession—that was regarded as the founding of the Japanese nation, though there is no historical proof whatsoever of the existence of Emperor Jimmu.

IKEDA: There was even a tendency to single out certain parts of the *Kojiki* from the rest of the text and use them to support the militaristic and antiforeign sentiments of the ultranationalists. An example is the following song associated with the name of Emperor Jimmu in the *Kojiki*. It belongs to a group known as "Kume songs" because they were handed down by the Kume clan:

> On the large rocks
> Of the sea of Ise
> Of the divine wind
> There are crawling around
> Shellfish—
> Like these, we will crawl around them
> And smite them relentlessly![3]

It is not surprising that the extremely uncritical and irrational methods exemplified in the treatment of texts such as the *Kojiki* before the war should have, by way of reaction, given rise to severe criticism in the postwar period. Even today, however, there are those who would interpret the *Kojiki* and similar texts in the old reactionary fashion and attempt to tie them in with Shinto organizations and the imperial system.

I certainly never want to experience again those nightmare times of the prewar period. I belong to the generation that grew up during the war and I know just how many young people were sacrificed in the cause of the ultranationalist ideology we have been discussing. After all, I can never forget that my four older brothers went to war, where one of them was killed. In addition, my house was burned down and my own health seriously impaired for a time. Therefore, in the past my impulse was always to reject the *Kojiki.* But with the passing of the years, my attitude has become more tolerant and forgiving of the past. I believe the time has come when we should reexamine the *Kojiki,* the oldest of all the Japanese classics, and try to understand and appreciate it correctly.

NEMOTO: There is probably no other classic of Japanese literature whose reputation has changed so radically over the years. In earlier centuries, the *Nihon shoki,* because it is more detailed and is included among the *Rikkokushi* (Six National Histories), was looked upon as the authoritative source for information on the ancient period, and the *Kojiki* was rather neglected. It was not until the rise of the so-called School of National Learning in the Tokugawa period (1603–1868) that the *Kojiki* was subjected to intensive study. Motoori Norinaga (1730–1801) produced a masterful commentary on it that served as the culmination of these labors, one of the most important scholastic accomplishments of the time. But he also laid the foundations for its eventual elevation to the status of a sacred text, one that is to be regarded as embodying absolute and incontestable principles of truth.

IKEDA: Yes. And then later, in recent times, as a reaction to such an approach, the historian Sōkichi Tsuda (1873–1961) and others have applied the principles of modern philological and historical criticism to the text. As a result of their researches, much of what is recorded in the work is no longer regarded as historical truth, but is viewed rather as myth and legend. Hence it has come to be almost entirely ignored by teachers of Japanese history in the postwar period.

NEMOTO: The whole process suggests how difficult it is to arrive at a correct appreciation and understanding of such texts of the ancient period.

THE BROADMINDEDNESS OF THE HUMAN DRAMA

IKEDA: First of all, there are of course many problems concerning the aims of the book and the methods by which it was compiled. The preface to the *Kojiki* says that it was compiled so that it could serve as "the framework of the state, the great foundation of the imperial influence."[4]

NEMOTO: The preface tells us that it was Emperor Temmu (r. 672–85) who first ordered the compilation of the work. Older texts known as the *Teiki* (Imperial Chronicles) and *Honji* (Fundamental Dicta) were to be purged of their errors and a true account fixed, so that it could be handed down to later generations. Emperor Temmu, the younger brother of Emperor Tenji, of course came to the throne only after emerging victor in the Jinshin Uprising of 672, in which he overthrew Emperor Tenji's son, who had claimed the throne on the death of his father. It is clear, therefore, that Emperor Temmu had political motives in mind when he ordered the compiling of a work of history, intending that it should prove his legitimacy and assert his right to become ruler.

IKEDA: The Jinshin Uprising was one of the most important events of the early period, one represented in the *Man'yōshū* by the works of such poets as Princess Nukata and Prince Arima.

NEMOTO: Yes. And it has also been pointed out that the Japanese rulers also wished to have a definitive account of the founding and history of the nation in order to strengthen their position in dealing with foreign nations. Japan at this time was establishing the so-called *ritsuryō* system of government, a bureaucratic system headed by the ruler and his court. This was the type of system already in effect in both China and the states of the Korean Peninsula, which had their own national histories, and the Japanese were anxious to follow suit. The *Nihon shoki,* which is written almost entirely in Chinese, is particularly strong in political and ideological coloring.

IKEDA: I am quite impressed with the fact that the early Japanese myths as they are recorded in these works seem so often to be more political in nature than those of ancient Greece, for example. It is also regrettable that none of the Japanese historical works of ancient times ever approached the scale of Chinese works such as the *Shih chi* (Records of the Historian) by

Ssu-ma Ch'ien (145?–90? B.C.), the first great historian of China. Ssu-ma Ch'ien's work, which covers the entire past of the Chinese people and the foreign peoples known to China, often presents highly critical accounts of the abuses and misrule of political figures and attempts also to describe the destiny of mankind as a whole. And yet even in the *Kojiki* there are passages that move beyond narrowly political concerns and deal with what we might call the broadmindedness of the human drama itself.

NEMOTO: This is a very important point to be noted if we are to appreciate the true value of the *Kojiki* as a classic of literature.

IKEDA: Political motives may have inspired the compilation of the *Kojiki,* and yet in some ways it fulfills its political aims rather poorly. It contains so many passages that seem to depart from strict political purposes and concerns.

NEMOTO: You are quite right. And, paradoxically, it is these very passages that give the work its literary importance and appeal.

IKEDA: One obvious example of this is the large number of ancient songs that are recorded in the *Kojiki.* In chapter ninety-eight, for instance, we find this song:

> Whoever it was
> Who brewed this wine
> Must have brewed it
> Turning his drum
> On one side for a mortar,
> While singing songs;
> He must have brewed it
> While dancing.
> That must be why this wine,
> This wine
> Is so extraordinarily enjoyable!
> —*Sa sa!*—[5]

The song is identified as a *saka-kura,* or wine-feast song. It is only a single example of such songs in the *Kojiki,* but one can see that it conveys the kind of interest one finds in *okagura,* the songs and dances of ancient Shinto. Yet delightful and interesting as it is, it would seem to represent rather a deviation from the supposedly political intent of the book.

NEMOTO: I agree that it doesn't seem to fulfill any particular political function.

IKEDA: And I would like to think that it represents not so much a conscious deviation from the political aim of the work as it does a simple and instinctive interest that the song and others like it aroused in the compiler. This, of course, is no more than a guess on my part. We are told in the preface that the *Kojiki* was written down by Ō no Yasumaro on the basis of recitations made to him by Hieda no Are, though I tend rather to think that it was the result of a number of compilers working together. However that may be, it would appear that the compiler or compilers were not content simply to assign political motivations to the various legends and other materials handed down to them and arrange them in simple chronicle form. Again I am merely guessing, but I wonder if they did not find themselves becoming engrossed in the drama of human history as a whole. I think that what we see in the *Kojiki* is the birth of a literary spirit that is responding to broader concerns of such a kind.

NEMOTO: That is an interesting suggestion. And indeed, if we consider the *Kojiki* in this light, it does have a clear and definite literary cast to it.

IKEDA: The *Kojiki* in fact abounds in anecdotes and passages that have very little political significance. An example that comes immediately to mind is the tale in chapter twenty-one of the white rabbit of Inaba. According to this legend, a rabbit who was living in the island of Oki wished to cross over the ocean to the mainland. He asked a *wani,* or shark, of the sea to call together all his shark relatives, saying that he wished to count how many of them there were. When the sharks were all lined up head to tail, the rabbit, pretending that he was counting them, raced over their backs and thus reached the mainland. Realizing that the whole thing was a deception, the last shark seized the rabbit and stripped him of his fur, but the deity Ōkuninushi, who happened along at the time, instructed the rabbit how to cure his wounds and regain his coat of fur. I remember we had to reenact the legend at one of the assembly programs when I was in elementary school. I wasn't assigned the part of Ōkuninushi. Instead I played one of the sharks who were deceived by the rabbit.

NEMOTO: It must have been a splendid performance, though it's too bad you didn't get to play Ōkuninushi!

IKEDA: Oh no, I'd much rather be just a plain human being than a deity. As one can see, however, the tale seems to have very little political significance. I would guess it was recorded because the compilers had a literary interest in such legends and traditions of the past.

THE UNIVERSALITY OF ANCIENT JAPAN

IKEDA: If we look into its origins, we find that it is in fact a folk tale of a kind that occurs rather widely. It happened to be included in the *Kojiki* because it became associated with the myths surrounded the figure of the deity Ōkuninushi. Tales of a similar kind are found in Korea, for example.

NEMOTO: Yes. In the "Tung-chuan" (Account of the Eastern Barbarians,), chapter 115 of the *Hou Han shu* (History of the Later Han), we find a similar story associated with Tung-meng-wang, the mythological progenitor of the Korean state of Koguryŏ. Pursued by his enemies to the bank of a river, he shot an arrow into the water, whereupon all the fish and turtles in the river came together and formed a bridge so that he was able to cross over and escape to safety.

IKEDA: Chapter nineteen of the *Kojiki* records another famous legend telling how the deity Susano-o no Mikoto, after being expelled from heaven by the other deities, descended to the region of Izumo. There he found an old couple who were weeping because an eight-tailed dragon had devoured seven of their eight daughters and was about to devour the last. Susano-o no Mikoto thereupon slew the dragon with his sword and rescued the maiden. This type of tale is of course very widespread in folklore. The Greek myth of how the hero Perseus rescued Andromeda, who had been presented as a sacrifice to a dragon, is an obvious example. Tara Ōbayashi, who is a specialist in comparative folklore, believes that such legends first appeared in the West around the middle of the first millennium B.C. They were apparently associated with the making of swords and the use of iron and gradually spread east to Asia.

NEMOTO: The legend of how the descendant of the sun goddess came down from heaven to a mountaintop in Kyushu closely resembles the tale of Tangun, the mythological progenitor of the Korean people, recorded in the historical work known as the *Samguk yusa* (Remnants of the Three Kingdoms).

IKEDA: Legends of that kind, too, seem to be very numerous. The Meiji-era (1868–1912) scholar and critic Chogyū Taka-yama (1871–1902) noted a number of similarities between Japanese and Polynesian legends, and on that basis he argued that the Japanese people are of a southern origin.

NEMOTO: Yes. The legends concerning the descent of the pro-genitor of the Japanese people from heaven seem to represent a mixture of elements, some typical of the nomadic peoples of northern Asia, others associated with the rice-growing peoples of the south. On this basis, scholars have offered various speculations as to where the Japanese people came from and the route by which such legends spread to Japan.

IKEDA: It is certainly difficult to determine the origin of the Japanese on the basis of such legends alone. And yet there is no denying that myths have a quite remarkable power to spread far and wide. But what interests me in particular is the universality of the men of ancient Japan, the way in which Japan resembles the world as a whole, we might say.

NEMOTO: When discussing such works of early literature as the *Kojiki,* it is more usual, of course, to emphasize the distinctive culture that they represent, to stress their indigenous elements.

IKEDA: Of course, we cannot overlook such elements. I have heard that there are also similarities between Japanese myths and Greek myths, and yet we cannot necessarily use these as proof that the two cultures have universal elements in common.

One can, in fact, only determine what elements in a culture may be universal in nature after one has finished examining the elements that are peculiar and indigenous to that culture. A text of ancient times such as the *Kojiki* would seem at first glance to be peculiarly indigenous, peculiarly Japanese in nature. To begin at once inquiring about what there is in it that is of universal or worldwide validity may appear to be rushing things.

I do believe, however, that any discussion of the indigenous elements of the text should be kept entirely free from the kind of ultranationalistic approach that seeks to glorify the imperial line and its eternal and unbroken succession, which, as the *Nihon shoki* puts it, is "coeval with heaven and earth."

NEMOTO: In other words, you would emphasize an approach that seeks to preserve and develop the independent and individual characteristics of a people or a region, and at the same time relates them to universal elements and characteristics.

IKEDA: Yes. Of course, this cannot be done in a simple, graphic manner. And yet myths would seem to represent a kind of crystallization of the experiences of men of ancient times. If we can transcend the barriers of time and place and somehow see into them and relive the experiences from which they arose, I believe they may lead us to a kind of human starting point that has meaning for men of all times and places.

Not long ago in the autumn of last year, I was traveling through the northwestern area of Japan. At that time I decided to visit the old Izumo region, which is associated with many of the myths we have been speaking of. As I was gazing out over Lake Shinji in Matsue, or again when I went to Hinomisaki Peninsula and looked out at the Japan Sea, I suddenly had a feeling that the men and women of those distant times had come back to life and were standing before me. The eternal validity and universality of the human story suddenly became for me an actual experience.

They say that in olden times, Lake Shinji was still connected with the ocean, and that the Izumo Shrine stood on an island in the ocean rather than on a part of the mainland, as it does now. The present shrine, though on the same site as the ancient one, is considerably smaller than the one that existed in those far-off days. And yet, according to the people of the area, it still preserves the atmosphere of the distant past.

In contrast with the Grand Shrine of Ise, which has so often been made use of for political ends, the Izumo Shrine seems to convey more clearly the air of mythical times, the true romance of human history. For that reason, I felt particularly reluctant to leave it.

GODS WITH HUMAN FAILINGS

NEMOTO: The *Kojiki* is divided into three books, the first dealing with the age of the gods, the second and third dealing with the age of human beings. And yet many of the accounts of figures pertaining to the so-called age of human beings, such as Emperor Jimmu, Empress Jingū, or Yamato Takeru no Mikoto, clearly contain many mythical elements. These mythical elements interspersed throughout the accounts of persons supposedly of a historical nature have given rise to much discussion among historians. Here, however, I hope we can deal with such accounts from a literary point of view, treating the *Kojiki* as a record of the human drama.

IKEDA: I agree that in the *Kojiki* there doesn't seem to be a great deal of difference between the age of the gods and the age of human beings. All the deities who appear in the *Kojiki* are limited to some degree in their powers and, in this sense, have a human quality to them. In the early pages of the book dealing with the age of the gods, we encounter Izanagi and Izanami, the original couple whose marriage produced various deities. They are followed by the sun goddess Amaterasu and her brother Susano-o no Mikoto. Through the episodes associated with these figures, we gradually see the world of human existence taking shape, with all its confrontations and troubles. Laughing, raging, weeping, rejoicing, jealous, suspicious—these are very human deities indeed.

NEMOTO: The myth of Izanagi and Izanami relates how the two are married and bring forth various children. The wife, Izanami, then dies and goes to Yomi, the land of the dead. Izanagi, filled with grief, visits her there but is frightened by the decayed state of her corpse and runs away. He is pursued by Izanami and other creatures of the land of the dead but manages to escape by throwing behind him three types of objects that change into other things. This theme of a flight in which one escapes by throwing down various objects that are transformed into other things occurs widely in the myths of many regions of the world. Even the fact that Izanagi threw down three objects coincides with versions of this theme in other mythologies.

IKEDA: This legend is particularly interesting because it has been interpreted as an attempt to explain the origin of death and divorce. In the story, the dead wife, Izanami, does not want anyone to see how ugly she has become. But in spite of her pleas, Izanagi lights a torch and looks at her. As he turns to flee, she pursues him, her former love for him giving place to hatred. He places a huge boulder in her path, blocking the passage at a spot called Yomotsuhirasaka. From the other side of the boulder, she calls to him, saying: "O my beloved husband, if you do thus, I will each day strangle to death one thousand of the populace of your country."[6] This has been cited as an explanation of the origin of death. I must say, however, that the scene of the husband fleeing from his wife has a certain contemporary ring to it.

NEMOTO: I suppose that once he caught a glimpse of the rotting corpse of his wife, all the love he formerly felt for her vanished. I can sympathize with the way he must have reacted.

Izanagi then cleanses and purifies himself, and various deities are born in the process. Most important of these are Amaterasu, the sun goddess, who is born when he washes his left eye; Tsukuyomi, the moon deity, born when he washes his right eye; and the god Susano-o, born when he washes his nose. These are the so-called three noble children, whom he assigns to rule over the lands of Takama no Hara, or the sky, the realms of the night, and the ocean, respectively. Susano-o, however, does not rule the area entrusted to him but instead weeps and howls.

IKEDA: It appears to have been a very violent fit of weeping and howling, something like a volcanic explosion. The text records that "his weeping was such that it caused the verdant mountains to wither and all the rivers and seas to dry up."[7] Susano-o is told that, because of his behavior, he is to be expelled from his domain. He goes to see his sister Amaterasu to take leave of her, but commits various outrageous acts that cause him to be expelled from her domain as well. After that, he descends to earth at Izumo. This passage seems to foreshadow a later episode in the *Kojiki* in which the ruler of the Izumo region agrees to cede his lands to the descendant of the sun goddess.

The god Susano-o is depicted as a young man who is given to fits of violent emotion and is one of the most interesting figures in the *Kojiki*. In some ways he reminds one of the hero of a modern novel. The novelist Ryūnosuke Akutagawa, in fact, wrote a fictionalized account of Susano-o, apparently because he was attracted by the manner in which the legends associated with the god give expression to the wild and impetuous side of human nature.

NEMOTO: These accounts of Susano-o are followed by the myths associated with Ōkuninushi, the deity of the Izumo region we have already talked about in connection with the story of the rabbit and the sharks. The Ōkuninushi legends seem to represent a combination of myths that were quite diverse in origin and belonged to different regions. Two main themes dominate the Ōkuninushi legends—that of the various ordeals that the deity had to undergo in order to achieve a position of dominance, and that of the love between him and his chief wife, the daughter of Susano-o, and his other wives,—and are often expressed in the form of songs. These legends, constituting one of the longest story sequences in the *Kojiki,* have been interpreted as reflections of ancient rites that accompanied initiation into manhood and rites associated with accession to rulership.

THE JAPANESE SENSE OF BEAUTY AND WORLD CULTURE

IKEDA: Whenever I read these legends pertaining to the age of the gods, I have the feeling that if the *Kojiki* was not treated as a Bible of Japanese nationalism but was, rather, approached in a freer and more imaginative manner, it might prove as rich a mine of stories of universal human validity as have the Greek myths. It seems a great shame to me that, because of its connections with the imperial family and the state in Japan, it has so often been shorn of the wings of imagination and shut away in a cage, as it were. The Greek myths, by contrast, have proved a source of inspiration to many modern writers, who have instilled these myths with new vitality and found in them a source for expressing timeless aspects of the human condition.

NEMOTO: The scholar Tetsurō Watsuji (1889–1960) produced comparative studies of the *Kojiki* and Greek mythology that are marked by very penetrating analysis. He finds that the people of ancient Japan display imaginative powers that are characterized by a tendency to become engrossed in the part at the expense of the whole. Thus he sees the Japanese myths lacking in the kind of rational, overall unity that marks Greek mythology. At the same time, he does discern a kind of unity of naive wonder and emotionalism that runs through the Japanese myths as a whole and gives them a literary effectiveness. He characterizes the descriptive passages of the *Kojiki* as displaying a wealth of intuitions but put together with a rather weak sense of overall unity.

IKEDA: Yes. Watsuji has characterized the Japanese myths as being weak in their lack of gravity or seriousness but impressive in the wealth of emotional expression they display. This strikes me as a very apt description of the literary nature of the *Kojiki,* and, indeed, of the main tendency of the Japanese literary tradition as a whole. Even in modern times, Japanese literature has tended to produce works that are distinguished not by their breadth of imagination or descriptive depth and power but rather by their intuitive beauty, freshness, and acuteness of sensibility.

NEMOTO: Watsuji has also pointed out that the opening passage of the *Kojiki,* which deals with "the beginning of heaven and earth," is remarkable for the vividly concrete and sensual quality of the description: "Next, when the land was young, resembling floating oil and drifting like a jellyfish, there sprouted forth something like reed-shoots. From these came into existence the deity. . . ."[8] It is certainly a highly visual and sensual type of description.

IKEDA: And these are the very qualities that are at the root of the Japanese poetic tradition. But if such qualities represent the temperament and particular nature of the Japanese, then I do not feel that we need lament because they have led to works that are small in scale or lacking in depth and seriousness. On the other hand, although I do not wish to disagree with Watsuji, I feel very strongly that the Japanese should not rest content with those qualities that have traditionally marked their art and literature and thereby devote themselves solely to the refinement of the kind of aesthetic sensibility represented by them.

At the present stage of cultural history, the traditional Japanese or Oriental type of aesthetic sensibility has much that it can contribute to the rest of mankind. But as I think about the century ahead and the future of world culture as a whole, I believe that Japan must take active steps to meet and mingle with cultural traditions that differ in nature from its own and that will add some of their richness to the Japanese tradition.

NEMOTO: Do you perceive elements in the *Kojiki* that differ from the traditional Japanese aesthetic sensibility?

IKEDA: That gets into a very difficult problem. History is irreversible, and even though we may discover in the past certain possibilities for development in directions other than the one that was taken, it is too late to do anything about them. We cannot experiment at this point to see where they might have led. However, I think we can say this: in our earlier discussions on the *Man'yōshū*, we noted that the anthology proved it was possible to have poetry representative of the common people. That possibility, however, was not pursued, and, as a result, popular poetry is almost entirely absent from the Japanese literary tradition in the centuries that followed. So I think we must recognize that the traditional Japanese artistic sensibility is something that was developed over a period of time through prolonged refinement and the rejection of elements and qualities that differed from it in nature.

I would venture to say that in ancient Japan—the Japan represented in the *Kojiki*—there existed elements quite different from the so-called sense of the transcience of life or the *mono no aware* (sensitivity to things) that is always said to characterize traditional Japanese literature. In works such as the *Kojiki,* we find a much more powerful and vital expression of the drama of life, I believe.

NEMOTO: I would agree with you that we must not always stick to the standard, accepted interpretations of the past. Specialists do not like people who put forth bold new theories. But such hypotheses are often useful and even necessary, especially when some new piece of evidence from the past is brought to light. We have seen an example of this only recently, when the discovery of the Takamatsu grave, with its startling murals, has thrown into doubt many of the accepted theories concerning life and art in the early period.

THE RIDDLES OF EARLY JAPANESE HISTORY

IKEDA: Up until now there has been no record of the existence of such tombs with mural paintings in Japan. Tombs of that type have been found on the Korean Peninsula, however, dating to the Koguryŏ state (?37 B.C.–A.D. 668) in the northern area.

NEMOTO: The Takamatsu tomb shows a much higher level of artistic development than do the rather primitively decorated tombs of the early period that have been known up till now. It was certainly influenced by Koguryŏ or Chinese models, and perhaps the relationship was an even closer one than mere artistic influence.

IKEDA: The person buried in the tomb seems to have lived in the *Man'yōshū* period, and scholars speculate that he or she may have been a member of the imperial family.

NEMOTO: It has been suggested, of course, that the ancestors of the Japanese imperial family may have come from Korea or China. Namio Egami has argued rather convincingly that a group of equestrian nomadic people from northeastern Asia invaded Japan through Korea sometime in the third or fourth century and imposed their rule over the country.

IKEDA: Schliemann's excavations of the ruins of Troy are another famous example of how earlier theories about the past were suddenly overturned. If some kind of archeological discovery were to be made that confirmed Egami's theory, it would certainly be an event of great significance.

NEMOTO: There are a number of problems concerning early Japanese history that continue to be the subject of much debate. Thus, speculation goes on concerning the location of the ancient Japanese state of Yamatai and its connection with the Yamato state in the Nara area; whether the sun goddess Amaterasu is to be identified with Queen Pimiko, who is mentioned in Chinese accounts of ancient Japan; whether Emperor Jimmu was a historical person or not; and so on. New hypotheses continue to be put forth, often of a sensational nature. Not only scholars, but the general reading public as well, appear to be fascinated with these riddles of early Japanese history. However, we seem to have wandered somewhat from the subject of the *Kojiki* itself.

IKEDA: Yes, I agree. In the first book of the *Kojiki*, which deals with the age of the gods, there is another very interesting legend, that of the brothers Umisachibiko (Luck-of-the-Sea Lad) and Yamasachibiko (Luck-of-the-Mountains Lad.) And in the second and third books we find other moving stories, such as that concerning Sahohime, the consort of Emperor Suinin, who was torn between love for her husband and for her elder brother, and that of Prince Mayowa, who, learning that his mother's second husband, Emperor Ankō, had murdered his father, killed the emperor in revenge. All these are superb tales, depicting real persons who are faced with dilemmas from which they can find no escape, described clearly and simply and presented in a manner that is deeply moving. But perhaps most impressive and fascinating of all is the tale of the hero Yamato Takeru no Mikoto, interwoven as it is with songs.

NEMOTO: Yes. The version of his story given in the *Nihon shoki* is by comparison much less colorful.

THE WORLD OF ROMANCE

IKEDA: The *Kojiki* presents with great force and effectiveness the drama of human beings who live to the fullest, and who fight and resist in the face of the overwhelming power of fate. Yamato Takeru can best be viewed, I believe, not as an actual individual, but as a heroic figure symbolic of the entire age, an embodiment of the emotions of the common people as a whole. It has often been suggested that his story represents a combination of a number of different hero legends. In his actions he is depicted as being "fearless and wild in disposition," [9] while the songs attributed to him reveal the naiveté and gentleness of his inner nature. We earlier quoted a song in which he urged the young men to wear oak leaves in their hair in order to secure long life. Another of the songs that he composed when he was recalling his homeland is even more famous:

> Yamato is
> The highest part of the land;
> The mountains are green partitions

Lying layer upon layer.
Nestled among the mountains,
How beautiful is Yamato! [10]

NEMOTO: Yamato Takeru, a son of Emperor Keikō, is repeatedly dispatched by his father to carry out campaigns of one kind or another. Thus he spends his adult years ceaselessly wandering from one region to another. His father was apparently afraid to have him at his side because of the prince's wild disposition. Thus, in order to insure the safety of the state, the prince was forced to live a life of hardship and sorrow.

IKEDA: On the surface, his story is certainly one of tragedy and eventual defeat. And yet I sense a note of victory in it, of praise for a man who, however oppressed by circumstances, continues to resist the established order as long as he is alive. His story is a prototype of what we today would call a romance.

NEMOTO: Although today the romance seems to be a lost literary form.

IKEDA: Unfortunately I am afraid that you are right. Novels such as *Ninety-three* and *Les Misérables* by Victor Hugo and *The Eternal City* by Sir Hall Caine are my favorites because they convey to me the true flavor of romance. To me there is nothing more beautiful, radiant, and appealing than the figure of a human being who, whatever the circumstances, never abandons his ideals or values, who longs for something eternal, and who continues to believe unflinchingly in the worth of concerted action. One must have faith in that quality in human beings that makes them continue to fight with all their might and struggle to overcome the obstacles that face them, no matter how cruel or ugly are the realities of the world in which they live. Without such faith and reliance, literature, history, and, indeed, all that we call human values and progress cease to have any meaning.

NEMOTO: I certainly agree with that. Nowadays there is a tendency to regard humanism or idealism as simply a form of ideology. And in the interpretation of history as well, we too often disregard human beings themselves and place undue emphasis upon the study of social environment, means of production, or economic questions.

IKEDA: And yet no one can deny the fact that it is human beings themselves who constitute the most important factor in the shaping and altering of the course of history. For that reason, we must keep our attention focused upon man himself, who is the chief actor, and judge all works of literature in that light.

Well, once more we seem to have strayed from the subject of the *Kojiki* itself. Perhaps we digress too freely, though I don't think that digressions are necessarily bad in themselves. In our next discussion, however, I hope we can consider the question of the *Kojiki* and its relationship with Buddhism, particularly with the *Lotus Sutra*.

❖ ❖ ❖ ❖ ❖ ❖ ❖ ❖ ❖ ❖ ❖ ❖ ❖ ❖

3. The *Lotus Sutra* and Japanese Mythology

❖ ❖ ❖ ❖ ❖ ❖ ❖ ❖ ❖ ❖ ❖ ❖ ❖ ❖

CULTURAL EXCHANGE IN THE ANCIENT WORLD

IKEDA: I have just been to Ehime Prefecture in Shikoku, my first visit there in seven-and-a-half years. From there I went through Tokushima and Kagawa prefectures and then returned here to Sōka High School for Girls in Osaka.

NEMOTO: That sounds like a strenuous schedule. Did you have a chance to visit Dōgo Hot Springs? It is a place that has many connections with the *Kojiki*.

IKEDA: No. I only got a glimpse of it from the car as we were going to Matsuyama.

NEMOTO: That's too bad.

IKEDA: However, although I did not get to the hot springs, I was much impressed with the poetic scenery, which gave me an unexpected feeling that I was traveling through the distant past.

I am always interested in the history and customs of the different places I visit, and when I have a few moments to spare, I like to recall them.

NEMOTO: Dōgo is a place famous in history. There is a legend of the deity Ōkuninushi associated with the hot springs, and Prince Shōtoku (572–621), among other well-known personages, is said to have bathed there.

IKEDA: The distinguished poet Shiki Masaoka (1867–1902), who was born in Ehime, has described its warm climate. It appears to have been famous from ancient times for its hot springs and beautiful scenery and was no doubt populated from a very early date.

NEMOTO: There are many dwelling sites in the area that date back to the Jōmon period, around 10,000 B.C.

IKEDA: Chapter six of the *Kojiki,* which describes a number of the islands that Izanagi and Izanami gave birth to, mentions it, saying: "Thus, the land of Iyo is named Ehime." [1] The passage first records that the deities gave birth to the island of Awaji, and next to the island of Shikoku, on which Ehime is situated. The order in which the lands are mentioned probably reflects the actual route by which people traveling from the Yamato region journeyed.

NEMOTO: That's an interesting suggestion. The *Kojiki* at that point perhaps mirrors the actual experience of the compiler. In our last session, I believe we decided to take up next the question of Buddhist influence in the *Kojiki.* Lafcadio Hearn (1850–1904) points out somewhere in his writings that a large number of the myths and legends of the world derive in some sense from Buddhism. I wonder if this is true of the Japanese myths recorded in the *Kojiki* as well.

IKEDA: That is a very important question. By seeking to answer it, I believe one can not only throw new light upon the universal nature of the *Kojiki,* but can also present a classic example of the way in which ideas and material objects pass from one culture to another.

Of course, the *Kojiki* is based mainly upon indigenous Japanese traditions. And yet I would like to believe that both Japan and other countries of the world in those early times were more open to cultural currents and exchanges with one another than we tend to think today. We in Japan have yet to overcome the narrowness of view imposed by the long period of isolationism in the seventeenth, eighteenth, and early nineteenth centuries.

NEMOTO: It is certainly a problem that requires breadth of view to be considered properly.

IKEDA: There are far more examples to prove the great extent of cultural exchange that took place in the ancient world than we could possibly go into here. But let me cite merely one of these, pointed out by the learned scholar Hajime Nakamura. He believes that Indian influence already existed in Japanese culture before the introduction of Buddhism in the sixth century. As proof, he points to the early Japanese word for rice.

NEMOTO: That sounds fascinating.

IKEDA: The ancient word for *uruchi,* or nonglutinous rice, was *urushine,* which derives from the Sanskrit *vríhi.* Another interesting point is that this Sanskrit word spread to the countries of the West and is the origin of the English word "rice." Thus the words uruchi and rice are both the result of a process of cultural influence that began in India.

NEMOTO: So even among the things we think of as most typically Japanese, we can find traces of the kind of disseminations you have been talking about. In those early times, when communication was far more difficult than it is today, it is almost miraculous to think that there should have been so much exchange between East and West.

IKEDA: And yet such a miracle actually did take place. And when we come to historical times, the evidence is even clearer. For example, the *Nihon shoki,* under the date A.D. 654, records: "In the summer, the fourth month, two men and two women of the land of Tokhara and one woman of Sāvatthī were driven by a storm to Hiuga."[2] The name Tokhara here seems to designate a kingdom on the lower reaches of the Mekong River, in present-day Thailand. Sāvatthī is probably the city of north-central India where the famous Jetavana Buddhist monastery was located.

These persons were evidently cast ashore in Japan by a shipwreck. In addition, there are many records of Buddhist monks who came to Japan from other countries. There were no doubt many different forms of cultural exchange and influence.

NEMOTO: We mentioned the scholar Chogyū Takayama and his comparative study of Japanese mythology a little earlier. If I recall correctly, he sees similarities between the deity Susano-o of Japanese myth and Indra, a hero-god associated with thunder and one of the most important deities of the Vedic religion of the Aryans of ancient India.

IKEDA: Yes. I believe most scholars now tend to deny that there is any connection between them. But I certainly admire Takayama for perceiving the similarities in the myths of the two gods.

NEMOTO: The fact that Indra was known as a thunder god, that he was noted for his bravery, and that he killed a dragon (called Vritra) are all points that he has in common with Susano-o. At the same time, Indra had a very wild and rowdy side to his nature, as seen in the tales of how he smashed the chariot of Ushas, the goddess of the dawn, or stole the wheels from the carriage of the sun god Sūrya. All these remind us of the violent deeds that Susano-o committed in the heavenly realm of his sister, the sun goddess.

IKEDA: Of course, the mere fact that there are points of resemblance in the myths associated with the two gods does not necessarily mean that one derives from the other. They may be quite separate in origin. And yet there is certainly much about Indra that calls to mind the figure of Susano-o. Though there may be many problems involved in attempting to establish an actual connection, it is an important point to keep in mind in considering the possibility of cultural contacts between India and Japan in ancient times.

NEMOTO: Takayama put forth his hypothesis with the aim of inviting controversy on the subject, and that is, of course, what has resulted. It is impossible, however, to deny his significance as a pioneer in the study of such questions.

IKEDA: If we praise him too highly, though, the experts may laugh at us.

NEMOTO: Perhaps you are right. Maybe we had better not pursue the matter any further here. But let us turn from these general remarks on cultural exchange to the more specific topic of Buddhist influences.

PRINCE SHŌTOKU'S UNDERSTANDING OF BUDDHISM

IKEDA: One of the things to be noted immediately about Buddhism is the large number of Vedic deities that have been absorbed into it. Thus the god Indra, whom we have been talking about in connection with Japanese mythology, is regarded in Buddhism as a patron and protector of the Buddhist faith and is called Shakudai-kannin or Taishaku-ten in Japanese. Again, Tōri-ten, or the Heaven of the Thirty-three Gods, is a general term in Buddhism for the various deities, considered as a group, of the Vedas.

NEMOTO: Vedic influence is evident in Japanese folk religion as well. The Shinto shrines known as Suitengū in Kurume and elsewhere are dedicated to the Vedic god Varuna. He entered Japan by way of Buddhism, in which he is known as Suiten and depicted as a god of the water. Later he came to be worshiped in Shinto shrines. Another Indian deity very widely worshiped in Japan is the goddess Benten, or Benzaiten, who also came in through Buddhism. In the Vedas she is known as Sarasvatī and is associated with lakes and rivers.

IKEDA: Another very popular deity in Japanese folk religion is Daikoku, the god of riches. Like Benten, he is one of the so-called seven deities of good luck. His name, which means "Great Black," is in fact a Chinese translation of Mahākāla, one of the names for the Hindu god Shiva. In Japan he has become associated with the deity Ōkuninushi, whom we have talked about earlier, because the ideographs for Ōkuninushi's name may also be pronounced Daikoku. Still another important god in Japanese folk religion, Kompira, the guardian of ships and seamen, was called Kumbhira in India and represents a deification of the crocodiles of the Ganges River. All of these figures, as you can see, have undergone considerable transformation in their progress from India to Japan.

NEMOTO: Returning to the subject of Buddhism and the *Kojiki,* the latter would seem to have been compiled about a century and a half after the introduction of Buddhism to Japan. The official date for that event is usually regarded as 538, though it is natural to suppose that some knowledge of Buddhism had been brought to the country earlier by immigrants from the mainland.

There is a type of grave found in Japan known as a *kamadozuka* that dates from the sixth century. It is clear that cremation was practiced by the persons who built such graves, and thus the Buddhist custom of cremation had already by this time been transmitted to Japan.

IKEDA: Even though certain Buddhist practices may have been

introduced, it was much later that a true understanding of the higher principles and teachings of the religion actually filtered down to the common level.

I would like to point out the fact that, where we find the exchange of ideas or the spread of a system of thought from one culture to another, there is always a pioneer figure, a leader of more than usual foresight who takes the initiative in promoting the process. Unless there is an individual who is willing to devote his life to the task—working to create a climate that is receptive to the new ideas, laying down a firm basis, harmonizing them with elements in the indigenous culture, and combating the native hostility that they at first arouse—then there can be no successful cultural exchange, no real progress of civilization.

NEMOTO: In the case of the introduction of Buddhism to Japan we would surely have to cite Prince Shōtoku as the earliest of such great pioneers. In recent years, however, scholars have begun to question many of the accomplishments traditionally attributed to him. Thus, for example, there are those who deny that the famous Seventeen-Article Constitution is actually his composition, and they also question his authorship of the *Sangyō-gisho,* three commentaries in Chinese on the *Lotus Sutra, Vimalakīrti Sutra,* and *Sutra of Queen Shrimālā,* respectively.

IKEDA: In the past the figure of Prince Shōtoku has been so extravagantly idolized that such an iconoclastic reaction was perhaps bound to occur. It is part of the general trend of our age to reevaluate the famous personages of the past. But if we deny all the accomplishments attributed to Prince Shōtoku, we can hardly hope to understand his significance as a historical figure.

There are many problems involved in judging his life and career correctly. With regard to the *Sangyō-gisho,* the theory put forward by Tatsunosuke Ōno seems to me to be most convincing. He argues that the commentaries were in fact compiled by Prince Shōtoku but were transmitted orally to his students, who then wrote them down.

However that may be, there is ample evidence to prove that Prince Shōtoku had a truly extraordinary understanding of Buddhism.

NEMOTO: After the prince's death, his consort, Tachibana no Ōiratsume, was supposed to have embroidered a mandala depicting a land called Tenju, or Heavenly Life. The embroidery is still preserved in the Chūgū-ji, a nunnery in the Nara area. I wonder what your opinion is regarding the region called Tenju? Some scholars interpret it to be the Pure Land of Amida, others the Pure Land of the Bodhisattva Miroku, or Maitreya.

IKEDA: There is no doubt that beliefs concerning the Western Paradise, or Pure Land of Amida, had already been introduced to Japan by this time, and the worship of the Bodhisattva Miroku also seems to have been widespread. But, in view of the fact that Prince Shōtoku, in his expositions of Buddhism, accorded the place of highest honor to the *Lotus Sutra,* I would like to interpret the mandala as a depiction of the Pure Land of Ryōzen, or Vulture Peak, the place in India where Shākyamuni preached the *Lotus Sutra.* That would appear to me to be the most appropriate interpretation in view of Prince Shōtoku's own beliefs.

NEMOTO: Some scholars have suggested that the land of Tenju is meant to stand for India itself, which was known in early Japan by the name Tenjiku.

IKEDA: That's an interesting suggestion. But I do not think that Tenju and Tenjiku are merely two versions of the same word. Basically, I believe it is more appropriate to view Tenju as an idealization of the realm of India, the site of the Vulture Peak where the *Lotus Sutra* was preached.

NEMOTO: Yes. That seems to be a very satisfactory explanation.

THE INTRODUCTION OF BUDDHISM AND
THE COMPILATION OF HISTORY

IKEDA: Once again, we have strayed from the subject of the *Kojiki*. But it is a necessary digression if we are to understand the circumstances under which that text was compiled. I say this because it is likely that the texts—the *Teiki* and the *Honji,* also called the *Kuji* (Ancient Dicta), both of which we mentioned earlier—that preceded the *Kojiki* were themselves influenced not only by standard Chinese historical works, but by Buddhist texts as well.

NEMOTO: According to the *Nihon shoki,* in the twenty-eighth year (A.D. 620) of Empress Suiko's reign, Prince Shōtoku, in concert with Shima no Ōomi (Soga no Umako), drew up works called the *Tennō-ki* (Record of the Emperors), *Kokki* (National Records), and others. This is the earliest mention we find of the compilation of historical records in Japan.

We may surmise, however, that actually there had been considerable progress in the compilation of historical records previous to this. In the fifth century, many immigrants came to Japan from the mainland, among them no doubt a number who could write Chinese and keep records of events. Moreover, Chinese historical texts preserve a memorial written in Chinese and sent by "Bu, the King of Wa" (presumed to be Emperor Yūryaku, r. 456–79) to the emperor of the Liu Sung dynasty (420–79) in China. This is further proof that there were persons at the Japanese court who could compose documents in Chinese. By the time of the reign of Empress Suiko, as we know from relics of that period, the Japanese were not only writing in Chinese but also using Chinese characters as phonetic symbols to record the Japanese language. It would appear that the *Kuji,* which constituted the main source for the Japanese myths recorded in the *Kojiki,* was committed to writing sometime during the period from the reign (?507–31) of Emperor Keitai to the reign (539–71) of Emperor Kimmei. It is a fact of great interest that this is precisely the period during which we find the first official notice of the introduction of Buddhism to Japan.

IKEDA: Even before the introduction of Buddhism, I believe that Japan had already come under the influence of Indian culture. In fact, I would like to surmise that the ancient Japanese myths in the course of their transmission in this early period absorbed a rather large number of elements from India. Later, at the time when this body of mythology was being committed to writing, it was further influenced to a marked degree by Buddhism and the other elements coming into Japan with Buddhism.

It may appear as though I am trying to lay undue emphasis upon Buddhist influence for personal reasons, but that is not the case. In fact, it is only natural to suppose that such influence existed. The period from the reign of Emperor Temmu to the reign (708–14) of Empress Gemmei, when the *Kojiki* was attaining its final form, was, of course, one in which Chinese translations of Buddhist works were exercising a major influence upon forms of expression and ways of thought, and this influence could not help but be reflected in the *Kojiki*. This, I believe, is the way we can best sum up the situation.

NEMOTO: In other words, these Buddhist influences found their way into the text through its compiler, Ō no Yasumaro.

IKEDA: In our earlier discussions I observed that what I would like to see in Ō no Yasumaro's work is the beginnings of a literary spirit. And, as Hideo Kanda has very clearly and vividly pointed out, it was the Chinese translations of Buddhist texts that influenced Ō no Yasumaro most profoundly from a literary point of view, particularly the translations of the *Lotus Sutra* and the *Vimalakīrti Sutra*.

THE INFLUENCE OF THE LOTUS SUTRA
AND THE VIMALAKĪRTI SUTRA

NEMOTO: The Buddhist scriptures are noted for their wealth of imaginative power. The Japanese, stimulated by this aspect of Buddhist literature, were inspired to gather up the various myths and legends scattered in different regions of the country and weave them together in the form that they appear in the *Kojiki*.

IKEDA: If I may borrow the findings of Professor Kanda in his studies of the *Kojiki*, I would like to point out that both the style and construction of the *Kojiki* show marked influence from the *Lotus Sutra* and the *Vimalakīrti Sutra*. One of the features of the *Kojiki*, for example, is the skillful way in which ancient songs have been woven into the text. These, he believes, are imitated from the *ge* (*gāthā*) verses that are used in Buddhist texts to praise the Buddha or to sum up major points of doctrine.

The *Lotus Sutra* makes very frequent use of such verses. These follow prose sections of the text and are introduced by the formula: "Thereupon so-and-so, wishing to repeat what he had said, sang in gāthās." There then follows an extended passage that repeats in rhymed form the meaning of the prose section. This type of literary form, which combines prose and verse sections, has its origins in the Vedas, the earliest religious texts of ancient India. The form was taken over in Buddhist writings and spread east to China and Japan with the Buddhist religion itself. I find this a highly interesting and significant suggestion.

NEMOTO: I agree with you.

IKEDA: The rhythmical, flowing style of the *Kojiki* reflects the fact that the text, or the sources upon which much of it is based, was transmitted orally. In this respect it has much in common with the early Buddhist scriptures.

In the middle section of the *Vimalakīrti Sutra* there is a long passage in which, the lay believer Vimalakīrti having fallen ill, the Buddha requests various of his disciples and Bodhisattvas in turn to go to visit Vimalakīrti and inquire how he is. Each person requested then relates some experience that he has had in the past with Vimalakīrti and declines to undertake the mission on the grounds that he is unworthy. The narrative makes use of formulaic elements that are repeated each time, such as the words "What is the reason for this?" followed by an explanation of why the person is unworthy of undertaking the mission. The explanation concludes with another formula, the words "Therefore I am not worthy to visit him and inquire about his illness."

Professor Kanda argues that there are many indications in the *Kojiki* that this question-and-answer format has been imitated from the *Vimalakīrti Sutra*. For example, in chapter seventeen, when Amaterasu has hidden herself in a cave and the other deities are attempting to lure her forth, she says: "But why is it that Ame no Uzume sings and dances, and all the eight-hundred myriad deities laugh?"

To this Ame no Uzume replies: "We rejoice and dance because there is here a deity superior to you." [3]

In this case, I believe we can say that the wording and style of the *Kojiki* clearly reflect the influence of the *Lotus Sutra* and the *Vimalakīrti Sutra*.

NEMOTO: To the best of my knowledge, the Chinese classics do not employ this kind of why-and-because formula to express causal relationship.

IKEDA: Again, in the *Kojiki* myths and legends, when someone addresses a deity or sovereign, the honorific verb *po* or *haku* is employed. This usage is almost certainly taken from the Chinese translations of Buddhist scriptures. Thus, for example, in chapter sixteen of the *Lotus Sutra*, "Nyorai juryōhun," we find the sentence: "Maitreya Bodhisattva and others said to the Buddha." In the Chinese text of the original, the word "said" is expressed by the verb po or haku. This use of the word po as an honorific verb meaning "to say" is, I am told, rarely found in the early Chinese classics.

THE USE OF CHINESE CHARACTERS AS PHONETIC SYMBOLS

IKEDA: In the *Kojiki,* Japanese songs and place and personal names are recorded according to a system by which Chinese characters are used purely for their phonetic value. This is a system that had been devised earlier in China to be used by translators when they wished to record non-Chinese names or words in Chinese characters. Thus we find it employed by Kumārajīva (344–413), the great Buddhist missionary from Central Asia, in his translations of the *Lotus Sutra,* the *Vimalakīrti Sutra,* and other scriptures. For example, chapter twenty-six of the *Lotus Sutra,* "Daranihon," contains transcriptions of Indian *dhāraṇīs,* or "spells," written in this system. In this instance, the influence of the Buddhist texts upon the *Kojiki* and its system of transcription would appear to have been definitive.

It is important to note that this system of transcription of foreign words, as well as the use of the honorific verb po, is already to be found in usage in the inscription on the stele that King Changsu of Koguryŏ set up in 414 in honor of his predecessor, King Hot'ae. Professor Kanda surmises that the practice of using Chinese characters for their phonetic value was transmitted to Japan over the following route: from Kumārajīva's translation of the *Lotus Sutra* to the inscription for King Hot'ae of Koguryŏ to the Korean kingdom of Paekche to the court of Empress Suiko in Japan to the *Kojiki.*

NEMOTO: In this early period, when Japan possessed no writing system of its own, it would, in fact, have been impossible to record Japanese songs or proper names if such a system had not already been in existence.

IKEDA: In using characters to represent foreign names or words, the Chinese customarily chose characters that were unusual and seldom found in ordinary writing so that they could be easily distinguished from characters used for their meaning. This was the practice adopted in Chinese translations of Buddhist texts as well. Thus, in the *Lotus Sutra* we find that the Chinese characters used to represent words such as *arhat, ashura, pāramitā, upāsaka*, or *sahā* are quite different from the general run of characters one would encounter in the Confucian Classics. In representing Japanese sounds, the *Kojiki* uses exactly the same set of characters as those used in the *Lotus Sutra* to indicate the sounds of Sanskrit, Pali, and other non-Chinese languages.

NEMOTO: Is that so? Then this is a clear case of the influence of the *Lotus Sutra*.

IKEDA: There are many points at which the diction of the *Kojiki* also seems to have been influenced by the *Lotus Sutra*. For example, in chapter thirty-five, when Ōkuninushi is being pressed to surrender his land, we read: "Thereupon, these two deities descended to the beach of Inasa in the land of Izumo, unsheathed a sword ten hands long and stood it upside down upon the crest of the waves; then, sitting cross-legged atop the point of the sword, they inquired. . . ."[4] The characters used to express the idea "sitting cross-legged" are *fuza*, the latter part of the term *kekka-fuza* employed in the *Lotus Sutra* to designate the cross-legged sitting posture adopted by the Buddhas when in meditation.

In addition, the *Kojiki* term *jōshin* (to become a deity) seems to have been modeled on the Buddhist term *jōbutsu* (to become a Buddha). And various other terms, including such words as *kangi* (bliss), *hinkyū* (poverty), *shitto* (jealousy), and *yūgyō* (to wander), all appear in the *Lotus Sutra* and may well have been borrowed from it.

NEMOTO: In terms of the people of the time, then, these were all foreign loan words. They seem like perfectly natural Japanese words to us today, but to the men of ancient times they must have had a very fresh and unusual sound.

IKEDA: Just as educated Japanese of the Meiji era who had studied European thought and culture used words borrowed from German or English in their speech, so the men of ancient Japan must have employed new terms that they had learned from Chinese translations of the Buddhist scriptures.

ANALOGIES WITH KUMĀRAJĪVA'S TRANSLATIONS OF BUDDHIST SCRIPTURES

NEMOTO: However that may be, I wonder just how much understanding of Buddhism Ō no Yasumaro, the compiler of the *Kojiki*, really had.

IKEDA: We have no other evidence than the *Kojiki* itself to determine how well Ō no Yasumaro was acquainted with Buddhism. And we must keep in mind that Buddhist influence may have come into the materials from which the *Kojiki* was compiled at an earlier date. It need not necessarily be attributable to Ō no Yasumaro alone.

I would like here to speculate on the influence that Prince Shōtoku may have exerted upon the *Kojiki*. As we have noted, Prince Shōtoku was an expert on the *Lotus Sutra* and the *Vimalakīrti Sutra* and is said to have compiled commentaries on them. After his time, I wonder if the educated persons associated with the Japanese court were not more or less expected to have a knowledge and appreciation of these texts.

NEMOTO: The Ō family in later times became known as hereditary masters of Gagaku, a type of court music and dance. It is reasonable to suppose that they had frequent opportunity to come into contact with foreign culture. Ō no Yasumaro's preface to the *Kojiki*, however, reveals mainly his acquaintance with Confucian learning.

IKEDA: Probably his basic education was in the Confucian texts. And he also had some connection with families who were hereditarily in charge of affairs pertaining to the Shinto deities. And yet he must have worked very hard at his labors as a compiler and struggled with many problems relating to the style and organization of the text. In the course of these exertions, I believe he must have acquired a considerable knowledge of Buddhist texts and gained a rather deep understanding of the Buddhist spirit. And I believe that there is evidence to prove my assumption.

NEMOTO: Do you mean that in adopting phrases and modes of expression from the Buddhist scriptures he to some extent absorbed their content at the same time as well?

IKEDA: Yes. In a sense, the task that he performed in compiling the *Kojiki* was similar to Kumarajīva's labors in translating Buddhist scriptures into Chinese. The *Fo-tsu t'ung-chi,* a collection of biographies of early Indian and Chinese Buddhist monks written in Chinese, tells us something about the system employed for translating Buddhist scriptures at the time of the Liu Sung dynasty. There were nine persons involved in the process of translation, each with his fixed duties. First was the "translation master," who read the Sanskrit text aloud. Then came the "expounders of the meaning," who explained what the text meant; the "recorders" and others, who translated the text into Chinese; and finally a number of "collators" and "polishers," who made certain that the translation agreed with the original in meaning and that it was in smooth Chinese. Thus the translation of a single Buddhist text involved the cooperative labors of a number of different persons.

Ō no Yasumaro is said to have written the *Kojiki* on the basis of recitations of earlier texts made to him by Hieda no Are, and there were undoubtedly other persons involved in the process of compilation as well. Thus I would surmise that the process by which the *Kojiki* was compiled was not very different from that used in the translation of Buddhist scriptures into Chinese.

THE NIHON SHOKI AND THE SUTRA OF THE GOLDEN LIGHT

NEMOTO: The *Nihon shoki*, written in Chinese and completed shortly after the *Kojiki*, appears to have been much influenced by the *Sutra of the Sovereign Kings of the Golden Light Ray*, particularly the Chinese translation by the T'ang-dynasty priest I-ching.

IKEDA: Yes. It has frequently been pointed out that the style and phrasing of the *Nihon shoki* show the influence of Chinese historical works such as the *Han shu* (History of the Former Han) and the *Hou Han shu* or of literary anthologies like the *Wen hsüan* and the *I-wen lei-chü*. But it is clear that the authors also drew upon the *Sutra of the Golden Light*, as the work you have mentioned is commonly referred to. For example, in the section dealing with Emperor Kenzō (r. 485–87), an old woman named Okime implores the emperor to give her permission to return to her home, saying: "My strength has waned away. I have grown old and emaciated; even leaning on a rope, I cannot make my way forward." This passage, as has been pointed out, is based upon the *Sutra of the Golden Light*, section twenty-four, "Getting Rid of Illness," the sentence that reads: "I have already waned away, I have grown old and emaciated; even leaning on a stick I still cannot make my way forward."

NEMOTO: That is certainly interesting. The sentence has been taken over almost verbatim.

IKEDA: Though both the *Kojiki* and the *Nihon shoki* were influenced by Buddhist works such as the *Lotus Sutra*, the *Vimalakīrti Sutra*, and the *Sutra of the Golden Light*, the difference between them is comparable in a way to the difference between the *Lotus Sutra* and the *Sutra of the Golden Light*. Both the *Sutra of the Golden Light* and the *Lotus Sutra*, of course, give expression to the doctrines of Mahayana Buddhism. And yet the content of the Truth expounded in them differs clearly in degree of depth and loftiness in a way that cannot be overlooked.

NEMOTO: The *Sutra of the Golden Light* enjoyed particular favor during the reign of Emperor Temmu and was honored principally as a sutra that insures the protection of the nation.

IKEDA: Of course, the *Sutra of the Golden Light* is an important expression of Buddhist teaching. It is not concerned merely with doctrines pertaining to the protection and preservation of the state. And yet it is a provisional statement of doctrine that belongs to the Nizen period, the period prior to the expounding of the *Lotus Sutra*. Therefore it lacks the philosophical profundity of the *Lotus Sutra*, which expounds the principle of the eternal life force.

NEMOTO: As I recall, Nichiren Daishōnin (1222–82) often quotes from the *Sutra of the Golden Light* in his *Risshō ankoku ron* and other works.

IKEDA: Yes. He of course views it from the highest level of understanding and in that spirit cites it as an aid in the explanation of Truth.

NEMOTO: This may be slightly off the subject, but I wonder if you could explain to me how deities such as Amaterasu are viewed in Nichiren Daishōnin's system of Buddhism?

IKEDA: I have discussed that question elsewhere, but I will sum up my remarks here. First of all, one must realize that in

Buddhism *kami* (deities) are not regarded as transcendent or omnipotent beings. They are looked upon as functions or manifestations of the life force that is inherent in the forces of nature, the regions of the world, and the universe as a whole. The life force is the essence, the deities are the manifestations. Buddhism, of course, is concerned primarily with expounding the philosophy of the life force.

Thus Amaterasu is looked upon as that activity of the life force that absorbs energy from the sun and causes all living things to grow and flourish. The view, therefore, is essentially very different from that in Shinto, where Amaterasu herself is venerated as an object of worship.

It may be of interest to mention here the Buddhist interpretation of Hachiman, the patron deity of the warrior class. In terms of the philosophy of the life force, he represents the life force of the country or the land. The word *hachi,* or eight, is taken to be symbolic of the eight petals of the lotus, and hence of the *Lotus Sutra* and the Dharma. The character for *man* can be broken down into characters meaning cloth, rice, and paddy. Thus, in terms of Buddhism, Hachiman represents the power or functioning of the land, which causes the crops to grow and enriches life.

NEMOTO : In other words, the various activities of the life force in the universe are likened to kami.

THE MEANING OF THE WORD "LITERARY"

IKEDA : I think that is the way you can put it. But to return to the subject of the *Nihon shoki,* I believe we can say that the compilers of that work manifested a particular interest in the *Sutra of the Golden Light* and borrowed heavily from it because the sutra is similar in its general aim and orientation to the the *Nihon shoki.* In our earlier discussions we pointed out that, while the

Kojiki is essentially humanistic and literary in nature, the *Nihon shoki* tends to be more political and ideological. This may be something of an oversimplification, and yet there is no doubt that the two texts differ somewhat in their outlook. I wonder if these differences are not reflections of the differences in the respective Buddhist texts that influenced them.

NEMOTO: There is no doubt that, among all the various sutras, the *Vimalakīrti Sutra* stands out for its unusual literary interest. As has been pointed out, the text reads almost like a novel. The *Lotus Sutra*, too, has exerted great influence upon many works of literature.

IKEDA: Yes. But when we speak of the literary element or interest in a work, I hope we do not simply mean its form and manner of expression. I would like to interpret it in the more fundamental sense of a work that seeks to explore the meaning of human existence, to discover what is at the very core of life.

The Mahayana sutras, and the *Lotus Sutra* in particular, have exerted an enormous influence upon Japanese literature. I hope in our forthcoming discussions that we can examine this influence in more detail. But I am afraid that if we do not first understand the essence of Buddhism itself and the true nature of the *Lotus Sutra*, our discussions will never go beyond a superficial level.

NEMOTO: That is an important point. There are still many problems relating to the *Kojiki* and its mythology that I wish we could take up. We have not gone into one of the most interesting of them—namely, the difference in character between the myths associated with the Yamato region and those associated with Izumo, and the manner in which the various groups of deities have been combined. In addition, there is the theory put forward by folklore specialists that sees the myths of the *Kojiki* as reflections of certain religious ceremonies conducted by the court, such as the *chinkonsai* (spirit-pacification ceremony) and the *daijōsai* (great thanksgiving ceremony), and performed at the accession of a new emperor. I would like to have discussed this theory, as well as to have explored the political background of the period that produced the *Kojiki* and the *Nihon shoki*.

IKEDA: I'm afraid that if we try to take up too many problems, we will never come to the end of our discussion.

NEMOTO: Perhaps you are right. We had better end our session here.

PART THREE

The World of *The Tale of Genji*

❖ ❖ ❖ ❖ ❖ ❖ ❖ ❖ ❖ ❖ ❖ ❖ ❖ ❖

4. Poetry and Realism in Heian Literature

❖ ❖ ❖ ❖ ❖ ❖ ❖ ❖ ❖ ❖ ❖ ❖ ❖ ❖

DESCRIPTIONS OF NATURE IN HEIAN LITERATURE

NEMOTO: The *Genji monogatari,* which will be the topic of our discussions here, is regarded as the greatest masterpiece of Japanese literature. Murasaki Shikibu (Lady Murasaki), its author, probably began writing around the period 1001 to 1006 and completed the work shortly before her death, which seems to have been around 1014. The book is in fifty-four chapters and is one of the longest and finest works of fiction in all of world literature.

In dealing with a work of such magnitude and importance, there are, of course, many aspects we will want to discuss. In view of the remarks we have made above, I wonder if we may begin by considering the question of the relationship between nature and human civilization as reflected in the novel.

IKEDA: That would be an excellent idea. As I was thumbing

through the book, I happened to come upon a passage that I would like to cite. It comes at the beginning of the chapter entitled "The First Warbler": "New Year's Day was cloudless. There is joy inside the humblest of hedges as the grass begins to come green among patches of snow and there is a mist of green on the trees while the mists in the air tell of the advent of spring. There was great joy in the jeweled precincts of Genji's Rokujō mansion, where every detail of the gardens was a pleasure and the ladies' apartments were perfection."[1]

The passage is unpretentious, and yet to those of us accustomed to the cramped and bustling world of today, it has an astonishing freshness and charm. We can see how deeply the hearts of the men and women of the Heian period (794–1185) were moved by the subtle changes of the natural world. Nature is not reduced to a mere physical phenomenon, but is looked upon as a vital manifestation of life. We are presented with a living, pulsing world in which man and nature blend, harmonize, and interact with one another.

NEMOTO: The seven chapters that begin with the one quoted above are entitled "The First Warbler," "Butterflies," "Fireflies," "Wild Carnations," "Flares," "The Typhoon," and "The Royal Outing." As these titles suggest, the chapters unfold the story in terms of the four seasons of a single year. I would guess that this type of construction, which uses the seasonal cycle as its framework, has few parallels in other works of world literature.

IKEDA: The author, Murasaki Shikibu, has carefully worked the various flowers and other objects of nature into the titles of her chapters. In reading Western novels, I often find the passages of natural description exceedingly long and tiresome. In order to avoid having them interfere with one's enjoyment of the story, I think it is many times better just to skip over them. In most works of Heian literature, however, the descriptions of nature seem in general to be closely harmonized and interwoven with the story itself, though of course there are exceptions.

NEMOTO: This is no doubt because, as we have observed, man and nature are regarded not as separate beings, but as a single entity.

IKEDA: Yes. The descriptions of nature are not presented merely for their own sake alone. They are more like descriptions of nature as it is perceived and internalized by the subject of the passage himself.

NEMOTO: The aesthetic sense that is displayed in works of Heian literature forms an important basis for the sensibility of the Japanese people as a whole. And if we inquire how this sensibility was formed and nurtured, we would have to say that it is greatly influenced by the seasonal changes that take place in the natural world. Another element in it is the seasonal awareness of an agricultural people whose lives are governed by the rhythms of spring sowing and autumn harvesting.

IKEDA: And I would add that this sensibility is at the same time further refined by the process of reacting to nature. We must recognize the richness and depth of the heart that is moved to response by the varied impressions of nature, its subtle patterns of color and shadow.

DELIGHTS OF THE FOUR SEASONS

NEMOTO: Which of the seasons is your favorite?

IKEDA: If I tell you, we may get into one of those traditional debates over which season is the finest. Prince Genji, the hero of the *Genji*, at one point says to one of his lady friends: "People have always debated the relative merits of the groves of spring and the fields of autumn, and had trouble coming to a conclusion." [2]

As Genji's remark indicates, it has been a tradition in Japan to debate over which is superior, spring or autumn. In chapter 107 of the *Kojiki* we find the story of two brothers named Haruyama no Kasumi Otoko (Youth of the Spring-Mountain Mist) and Akiyama no Shitabi Otoko (Youth of the Autumn-Mountain Crimson). These deities appear to be personifications of the spring mists and autumn leaves respectively. They engage in a contest for the hand of a young woman, and the young man from the spring mountain wins. And yet the Japanese temperament more often seems to prefer the autumn season.

The *Man'yōshū* contains a famous poem by Princess Nukada in which she decided a debate over which was superior, spring or autumn, by saying:

> But when on the autumn hill-side
> We see the foliage,
> We prize the yellow leaves,
> Taking them in our hands,
> We sigh over the green ones,
> Leaving them on the branches;
> And that is my only regret—
> For me, the autumn hills! [3]

And the *Shūishū*, an anthology of poems compiled on imperial command around 1005, contains an anonymous poem that reads:

> In spring it is the cherries,
> their blossoming alone
> we think of,
> but autumn is more filled
> with the sadness of things.

NEMOTO: In the poetry contests that were held so frequently during the Heian period, it was a favorite pastime to debate in verse over which is superior, spring or autumn. As contests of opinion go, they were certainly very mild and refined ones.

IKEDA: I suppose if I had to give an opinion, I would say that I am more attracted to autumn, though of course each of the four seasons has its own particular delights. The custom of debating whether spring or autumn is superior is in a sense symbolic of the deep-seated Japanese concern for the seasons as a whole and for the world of nature.

NEMOTO: The *Makura no sōshi* (Pillow Book) of Sei Shōnagon, another masterpiece of Heian literature, begins with a famous passage in which she discusses the different sights and interests aroused by the various seasons. It shows the same attitude you have been describing.

IKEDA: There is an interesting anecdote of a military leader of the sixteenth century who discussed men's personalities in terms of the characters of the different seasons. We today often speak of young people as so many "cherries, plums, peaches, and damsons," comparing them to the blossoms of these various trees and urging each one to develop the particular characteristics appropriate to him or her as an individual. This habit of drawing analogies from the seasons or the different varieties of flowers and plants seems to be peculiarly Japanese.

NEMOTO: That's an interesting point.

IKEDA: Again, the changes of the four seasons are often seen as symbolic of the various stages of human life. This type of analogy has its roots in Buddhist thought, I believe. Buddhism describes human life in the terms *shō, rō, byō,* and *shi* (birth, old age, sickness, and death), and these in turn are linked to the larger phases of coming into being, abiding, destruction, and return to emptiness that characterize all the phenomena of the universe. Thus the seasonal changes are seen as epitomizing the deeper meaning of the entire process of transmigration.

NEMOTO: The *Man'yōshū* very seldom mentions the beauties of winter. Perhaps the fact that winter becomes an important theme only in Heian times and later is due to the Buddhist influence you have mentioned.

IKEDA: Yes, I think so. The acute consciousness of death and impending change that comes to a person in his closing years is linked to the severity and melancholy of winter. And at the same time there is a sense of expectation and looking forward to warmth, just as, in the depth of winter, one has a sense of the spring and renewal of life that is about to come.

NEMOTO: There is a passage in the "Morning Glory" chapter of the *Genji* that deals with the winter landscape in the way we have been talking about:

"There was a heavy fall of snow. In the evening there were new flurries. The contrast between the snow on the bamboo and the snow on the pines was very beautiful. Genji's good looks seemed to shine more brightly in the evening light.

" 'People make a great deal of the flowers of spring and the leaves of autumn, but for me a night like this, with a clear moon shining on snow, is the best—and there is not a trace of color in it. I cannot describe the effect it has on me, weird and unearthly somehow. I do not understand people who find a winter evening forbidding.' "[4]

IKEDA: The passage represents the discovery of a new kind of beauty in the clear, serene landscape of winter.

THE OPPOSITION BETWEEN CIVILIZATION AND NATURE

NEMOTO: By comparison, people of our own time have become increasingly indifferent to the changes of the seasons. Not only that—we have gone even a step further and actually destroyed our natural surroundings in a heedless and deplorable manner.

IKEDA: I feel the same way. And as the feeling for the seasons and the world of nature is wiped out, people's hearts are at the same time reduced to a wasteland. The men and women of earlier times in Japan used to speak of "cherry viewing" or "maple viewing," words that carried with them a sense of refined and sensitive appreciation of the beauties of nature. Yet nowadays we are hard put to find any real cherry blossoms or autumn maple leaves to view and appreciate. The trees have withered or changed color as a result of the air pollution in the cities, and one must now go deep into the mountains before one can see the kind of cherries or autumn leaves that men of earlier times enjoyed.

NEMOTO: Our modern civilization, with its emphasis upon technology and economic growth, has exerted all its effort in the pursuit of endless progress and development. And as a result, the environment has been destroyed, natural resources are being depleted at an alarming rate, and men's emotional lives have in the end been impoverished and laid waste. The traditions of Heian literature should teach us that we must somehow recover what has been lost from our lives.

IKEDA: And yet that involves very difficult questions. I do not think our present dilemma can be solved merely by calling for a return to the past or to the state of nature.

When we examine the works of Heian literature, particularly such prose works as the *Genji,* we see that, in terms of the age, they are actually the products of a rather highly developed cultural milieu. Lady Murasaki and Sei Shōnagon, as well as the famous poets Izumi Shikibu and Akazome Emon, were all women in the service of the court. These women and others like them were in many ways the cultural leaders of the time and functioned as a kind of literary salon.

If we compare the poetry preserved in the *Man'yōshū* with that of the *Kokinshū* and other Heian anthologies, we see that there is a shift in the attitude toward nature. Whereas the poetry of the earlier period tended to be direct and active in approach, that of the later period is marked by a tendency toward indirection and abstraction. The simple and powerful tone of the *Man'yōshū* is increasingly lost, to be replaced by a growing artificiality and attention to technical dexterity.

NEMOTO: Yes, there is surely that side to Heian literature.

IKEDA: The description of the new palace that Prince Genji had constructed for himself, found in the chapter entitled "The Maiden," is a perfect example of this tendency. Genji has quarters designed for each of the four ladies whom he intends to have living there. The quarters are laid out in the four directions and correspond to the four seasons, with gardens for each, planted with trees and flowers appropriate to the season represented. Thus the passage reveals not only an awareness of nature but also a tendency to arrange and dispose it in accordance with a humanly conceived plan.

NEMOTO: In other words, it constitutes a kind of artificially created world of nature, something that would have been inconceivable to the people of *Man'yōshū* times.

IKEDA: Of course, it still represents an extension of nature itself and thus differs totally with the kind of alienation from nature that has come about in modern civilization. The advance of industrialization that has taken place in many countries in recent centuries has brought about far more rapid and drastic change than was ever known in the earlier centuries of human history. In many cases, the rate of change can only be described as extraordinary. And yet we must not overlook the fact that, whether slow or rapid, the advance of civilization is a process that brings with it certain inevitable results.

NEMOTO: Are you referring to the opposition created between nature and civilization?

IKEDA: Yes. And unless we recognize that such an opposition

exists, then all our criticisms of the modern age and of technological civilization will, I am afraid, result in a mere ineffectual nostalgia for the past or in dreams of a world that can never exist.

NEMOTO: I wonder if I may shift the direction of the discussion a little and consider for a moment the social background and actual way of life that gave birth to Heian literature.

The works such as the *Genji* that we have been talking about were written at the time when the Fujiwara clan was at the height of its power and, in fact, exercised complete control over the emperor and the government. Economically, it was a period when the great private land estates known as *shōen* were coming into existence. In other words, the old bureaucratic form of government and the economic forms that supported it were becoming increasingly ineffectual and meaningless. It was also a period when the learning and culture that had earlier been imported to Japan from the Asian mainland were being absorbed and adapted to Japanese tastes and needs.

POLITICS FROM THE COURT LADY'S POINT OF VIEW

IKEDA: There is one peculiar thing about the *Genji* that anyone reading the novel is almost certain to note. This is the fact that, although almost all of the characters are members of the imperial family or the aristocracy and hold positions of importance at court or in the government, there is little or no mention of politics or administrative affairs. Instead, the characters are depicted as though they did little else all day but compose poems and carry out their love affairs. Granted that the Fujiwara family at this time monopolized the power of government and it was a period of lasting peace, still the men at least must have had a certain number of other affairs that they had to attend to.

NEMOTO: The novel, we may say, reflects the outlook of the

women associated with the court, their isolation from politics and lack of interest in the subject.

IKEDA: The *Genji* is an undoubted masterpiece, and the diaries and memoirs of Lady Murasaki and other women writers of the time represent superb records of the actual thoughts and feelings of the writers. And yet, if we ask to what degree these writings reflect the true conditions of the time, we would be obliged to say that they represent only one remarkably narrow and isolated sector of Heian society as a whole.

For example, although it was a time of peace, we know from accounts in semihistorical works such as the *Ōkagami* that, in fact, there were constant struggles for political power taking place. The evidence indicates that it was a period of intricate scheming and ambition, of rivalry between the Fujiwara and Minamoto clans or among the various branches of the Fujiwara clan itself, and of plots on the part of the maternal relatives of the emperors to gain control of the throne.

NEMOTO: Of course, Prince Genji is depicted as going into exile to Suma and Akashi because of political intrigue.

IKEDA: Yes. But Genji's exile is voluntary and self-imposed. And after a few years he returns to the capital and eventually holds the highest position at court. In terms of the actual political conditions of the times, such an odd type of "exile" is quite inconceivable.

NEMOTO: In the novel, Genji's exile is described as having been made imperative because of his affair with a lady of the court named Oborozuki, though if we stop to consider this, it seems rather peculiar. It reflects the type of thinking characteristic of women like Lady Murasaki, who herself was a court lady, in which the withdrawal of a high minister from political life is treated as a problem arising from his private love affairs.

IKEDA: And yet it is just this manner of treatment that gives the *Genji* its literary purity, that allows it to create a world of fancy all its own. And if we look at the matter from another point of view, we would have to say that the private lives of statesmen often have quite marked effects upon their political careers.

Even today, as we know, wives who ostensibly are busy tending to household affairs can actually exercise a subtle and very telling influence upon the course of political and economic developments or upon the manner in which their husbands carry out their jobs. Women may tend to respond to problems less logically and more instinctively than men, and their responses therefore take somewhat different shapes. And yet women have a peculiar sensitivity in such matters that surpasses that of men.

NEMOTO: I agree with that entirely. And we must remember that the world of Heian Japan, particularly in the period dealt with in the *Genji*, was marked by a kind of isolationism. It was not the forced and stifling isolationism imposed by the shogun dictators during the Tokugawa period. Yet Japan as a whole was largely cut off and isolated from contact with the Asian mainland. And within this larger national isolation, the court aristocracy, which was concentrated almost entirely in the capital, Heian (Kyoto), constituted a tightly knit and closed society. Thus the works of literature such as the *Genji* that are the product of this society contain scarcely any description of the lives of the common people or the lower classes of Japanese society at the time.

IKEDA: It is true that here and there, as in the "Evening Faces" chapter, we have glimpses of the poorer sections of the city and the people living there, extraordinarily impressive, perhaps in part because, like scenes lit by a moon that appears briefly from behind the clouds, they come and go so quickly. But even such scenes are described with a sense of elegance and refinement. It is only in works such as the *Konjaku monogatari,* which we will be discussing later, that we have any feeling of the bustle and energy of the common people and get a real picture of their daily lives.

NEMOTO: The court ladies seem to have regarded the common people with distaste and horror. Sei Shōnagon remarks that she finds it somehow inappropriate to think that the snow should fall upon the houses of lower-class persons, or deplorable that the moonlight should shine into them.

IKEDA: Viewing the crowds of commoners who have gathered for a festival, the ladies are appalled by the confusion and feel as though they would like to push the rabble all aside. In a sense, the court ladies often display the temperament of parvenus, with a corresponding contempt for those of inferior social position. They were petted and made much of by those around them, and it undoubtedly went to their heads. And yet we must remember that the men and women of the time were acutely conscious of social position. It would be pointless for us, on the basis of the values of our own time, to accuse them of class prejudice.

THE SENSE OF IMPERMANENCE AND SPIRITUAL ANXIETY

NEMOTO: Their courtship and marriage customs were also completely different from ours.

IKEDA: As were their ideas about what constituted beauty in women. As Professor Kikan Ikeda has summed it up, the beautiful woman of Heian literature was expected to be pale, small in stature, round-faced, and somewhat on the plump side. In the *Genji,* ugly women are depicted as tall, skinny, and with large noses. Lady Suyetsumu, one of the uglier ones, was known as the red-nosed lady.

NEMOTO: Though their standards had something in common with ours, they apparently did not appreciate the type of slender, well-proportioned woman we are accustomed to admiring. They would not have understood our concepts of glamor or of women with cute, individual faces. They particularly admired long hair. A woman whose hair was so long that it trailed on the ground was singled out for special praise.

IKEDA: The women wore so many layers of clothing that the lines of their figures were completely concealed. As a result, all attention came to be focused upon their faces and hair and upon the kind of clothing they wore.

NEMOTO: The women certainly do not seem to have lived what we would call very healthy or active lives.

IKEDA: No. And that may be one of the principal reasons why Heian literature lays so much emphasis upon the inner life, the psychology of its characters. The women were very confined in their activities, spending almost all of their time cooped up within their chambers. They must have suffered from lack of exercise.

We tend to think of the men and women of the Heian court as living lives of great splendor and luxury. By modern standards, however, their manner of living was rather plain and drab. They had little in the way of fancy foods or drinks and no coffee or tobacco. Very likely they suffered from lack of proper nutrition. Their living quarters were quite open and exposed to the weather, so that they were very susceptible to illness.

NEMOTO: Listening to your remarks, I am beginning to lose my feeling of nostalgia for Heian times.

IKEDA: It is probable that their life span was on the average quite short. The *Genji* includes many impressive and deeply moving deathbed scenes. We notice that the women in particular have a tendency to die young. Making a quick check of some of the principal female characters in the novel, I find that Yūgao died at nineteen, Princess Aoi at twenty-six, Princess Rokujō at thirty-six, Fujitsubo at thirty-seven, Murasaki at forty-three, and Lady Oigimi, who figures in the last part of the book, at twenty-six.

In the "New Herbs" chapter we find a description of a ceremony held to celebrate the fortieth birthday of Prince Genji, which marks an important turning point in the development of the novel. From the elaborateness of the ceremony, we may surmise that one's fortieth birthday was looked upon as the completion of a cycle in the life of an individual.

NEMOTO: In later times it became customary to hold celebrations on the occasion of one's sixtieth and seventy-seventh birthdays, and there are plenty of people nowadays who live to see such festivities. The situation was, I suppose, quite different in Heian times, however.

IKEDA: And we must keep in mind that we are talking about a novel. From the point of view of literary effectiveness, it does not do to have one's heroines live to too great an age.

At the same time, the sense of spiritual unease and anxiety and of the impermanence of life that is so strong a characteristic in Heian literature probably has its origin in the actual conditions of the time. Men and women living such shut-in lives, often poor in health and seeing their companions die at an early age, could hardly have felt otherwise.

NEMOTO: That would seem reasonable.

IKEDA: One also notices how often the characters in the *Genji* are depicted weeping. The flood of tears becomes almost wearisome at times. They seem to respond with deep emotion to all the events of life, whether joyful or sad. This highly emotional temperament, too, I believe, was fostered by the sense of anxiety and impermanence we have been speaking of.

NEMOTO: And it was probably influenced to some extent by Buddhist concepts of the transience of life.

AN EMOTIONAL SENSE OF THE IMPERMANENCE OF LIFE

IKEDA: I hope we can discuss the relationship between the *Genji* and Buddhist thought a little later on. Here I think it is enough simply to state that, although the Buddhist doctrine of the impermanence of life may have deepened the feeling of spiritual anxiety that characterizes the *Genji,* it was not the source of that anxiety. The source of that anxiety and unease is the actual nature of human life, which cannot help but impress one with its transience.

When men and women face the fact of their own mortality, they may react in a number of different ways. What we find in the *Genji* is an attitude that seeks to confront each moment of life, conscious of its transience, to respond deeply to it, and to savor its particular essence. This attitude is charged with a greater emotionalism than the mere philosophical recognition of the impermanence of life. This is not the place to argue whether such emotionalism is superior or inferior to the more philosophical outlook. The point to note is that it constitutes a distinctive type of aesthetic sense that is deeply rooted in Japanese life and custom.

NEMOTO: And this emotionalism, I suppose one could say, forms the basis for the so-called *mono no aware,* or sensitivity to things, that is so often cited in discussions of Japanese aesthetics.

IKEDA: Yes, I think we could say that. But it seems to me there is a mistaken tendency to talk about both "the sense of impermanence" and "sensitivity to things" as though they were simply philosophical concepts. We must distinguish clearly between the "sense of impermanence" as a philosophical idea and the "sense of impermanence" as an emotional response. And I have a feeling that the term "sensitivity to things" also has two aspects to it, one philosophical and the other emotional.

NEMOTO: Motoori Norinaga, the great eighteenth-century critic of the *Genji,* showed profound insight in singling out "the sensitivity to things" as the outstanding characteristic of the novel. But, as you say, the exact meaning of the phrase is a problem that requires further study. Perhaps we had better postpone it until our later discussions.

Here I would like to consider some of the reasons why the Heian period saw this sudden and unprecedented appearance of works of literature written by women. The *Genji* is the most outstanding example, and we have already mentioned others, such as the *Pillow Book* of Sei Shōnagon.

First of all, we must take into account the factor of language and the writing systems in use at the time. The men, in drawing up documents and papers connected with the exercise of government, customarily employed the Chinese language, or a type of Japanese that made very heavy use of Chinese characters. The women, on the other hand, who did not have sufficient learning to write in Chinese, used the *kana,* or Japanese syllabary, for their own writings, and in the process succeeded in creating their own distinctive types of literature that are marked by great psychological subtlety.

IKEDA: It is certainly a fact of great interest that the women of the time, who were largely shut out of the world of politics and academic learning, should have become the creators of an entirely new kind of literature. It is also interesting that nearly all of these women writers were daughters of the lower aristocracy rather than women of the highest class. Thus, although they often served as ladies-in-waiting at court, they could view the court and the upper aristocracy with a certain degree of detachment.

NEMOTO: Undoubtedly a number of different factors contributed to the creation of this new literature.

IKEDA: One of them, which we should not overlook here, was the position that women held in the society of the time. As we have noted earlier, women had considerable freedom in matters of marriage, much more freedom than in later periods of Japanese history. But this freedom was accompanied by an element of uncertainty and instability.

NEMOTO: It was a polygamous society, there is no doubt about that. And yet men and women seem to have associated more or less on terms of equality and to have been relatively free in both matters of marriage and divorce. Thus we find women like the poet Izumi Shikibu, whose diary reveals that she was involved in marriages or love affairs with a rather large number of men. On the other hand, the *Kagerō nikki* (Gossamer Diary), written by the wife of a high official, indicates that, though the writer was a woman of great beauty and talent, her married life was marked by great uncertainty, neglect, and outbursts of jealousy.

IKEDA: Yes. Although we may speak of the men and women of the time as associating on terms of freedom and equality, it was not quite the same as today. I dare say there were no Sartres and Simone de Beauvoirs in the Heian period.

In the "Evening Mist" chapter of the *Genji* there is a passage in which Murasaki, moved by the fate of Lady Ochiba, muses upon the plight of women as a whole: "Such a difficult, constricted life as a woman was required to live! Moving things, amusing things, she must pretend to be unaffected by them. With whom was she to share the pleasures and beguile the tedium of this fleeting world?"[5] The passage symbolizes the fate that women must endure, regardless of what the marriage system may be, because of the realities of their social and economic position.

NEMOTO: The diary written by Lady Murasaki indicates that she herself was forced to undergo many bitter experiences.

HUMAN LIFE AND CREATIVITY

IKEDA: When I think about the trouble and melancholy that filled the actual lives of the women writers of the Heian period, I cannot but be impressed with the deep and mysterious relationship between the life of the individual and the act of artistic creation. The author of *The Gossamer Diary*, who is known to history only as "the mother of the General of the Right Michitsuna," writes at the end of the first chapter: "And so the months and the years have gone by, but little has turned out well for me. Each new year in turn has failed to bring happiness. Indeed, as I think of the unsatisfying events I have recorded here, I wonder whether I have been describing anything of substance. Call it, this journal of mine, a shimmering of the summer sky." [6]

The author of the *Sarashina nikki* (Sarashina Diary), who is known as "the daughter of Takasue," spent her childhood in rather humble circumstances in the provinces, enamored of the world of romance described in such works as the *Genji*. Her diary describes how she journeyed to the capital, entered service in the palace, married, bore a child, and eventually was widowed. Toward the end of this simple and restrained account of her life, she describes the loneliness of her late years in these words: "Many years have passed, but whenever I think about that sad, dreamlike time, my heart is thrown into turmoil and my eyes darken, so that even now I cannot clearly remember all that happened." [7]

The lives of these women, as well as that of Lady Murasaki, must, as far as women of that time went, have been fairly typical ones.

NEMOTO: And in spite of all the differences in time and circumstance and custom, the accounts of their thoughts and feelings that they have left to us ring with a note of true realism.

IKEDA: Lady Murasaki lived just at the time when the Fujiwara clan had reached the peak of its power and glory, as exemplified in the high official Fujiwara no Michinaga. But though Michinaga in his splendor was compared by his contemporaries to the full moon, the society that he represented was already beginning to show signs of decay. The reality described by the women writers of the Heian period represents only one narrow and isolated segment of the society of the time, the society of a Japan that was itself cut off from the rest of the world. And yet it is clear that these women, with their sharply realistic and penetrating vision, had already perceived the weaknesses that underlay the glory and splendor about them and were searching for the universal truths of human life. And the *Genji* stands as the highest achievement of that search.

❖ ❖ ❖ ❖ ❖ ❖ ❖ ❖ ❖ ❖ ❖ ❖ ❖ ❖

5. The Portrait of Prince Genji

❖ ❖ ❖ ❖ ❖ ❖ ❖ ❖ ❖ ❖ ❖ ❖ ❖ ❖

CULTURAL EXCHANGE WITH FOREIGN LANDS

NEMOTO: I understand you have just returned from a half month's visit to Hong Kong and Okinawa.

IKEDA: Yes. I came back to Tokyo for one day in between.

NEMOTO: You spent quite a lot of time going all around Okinawa. What were your impressions?

IKEDA: The island of Yaeyama, which is far to the west of the main island of Okinawa, was particularly impressive. There is something so rustic and exhilarating about it. It is very different in atmosphere from the main island of Okinawa. One feels as though the origins of the Japanese people were still alive there. I hope it can become something of a Hawaii for the rest of Japan. It has people, it has beautiful natural surroundings, it has stars—I fervently hope that all these can be preserved as they are now.

NEMOTO: I suppose you must have met a great many people in the course of your trip.

IKEDA: Yes. I received a very warm welcome, and I was able to convey my greetings to many people. It was an extremely meaningful experience.

NEMOTO: When we think of Okinawa, we immediately recall the terrible sufferings inflicted upon the people there during the Pacific War.

IKEDA: Well, the past is the past. In terms of Buddhist doctrine, it is the present and the future that are important. What counts is the manner in which men use the present as their basis and build for the future. At the gatherings of students that I addressed, I tried to stress that point and to encourage them to do their best.

NEMOTO: I see.

IKEDA: I came away from my trip with one other strong impression: I was struck by the great importance of cultural exchange and mutual understanding among areas that differ in culture and customs. Up to now, in considering the relationships between Okinawa and the main islands of Japan, or between Japan and the countries of the Asian mainland, too much stress has been placed upon political and economic aspects. Such an approach can never lead to true understanding and meaningful exchange. I think it is far more important to try to deepen knowledge and understanding in matters concerning language, folk customs, and religion. This may appear to be a roundabout approach, but I think it is the quickest route to the goal we are seeking.

NEMOTO: And I suppose you would include literature and the arts in the subjects to be stressed, particularly the classical works of literature.

IKEDA: Yes, of course they would be included.

NEMOTO: In that case, our own discussions of the classics, roundabout as they may seem, are quite justified.

IKEDA: I surely hope so! In approaching the classics, we learn to transcend the barriers of time and to discover and appreciate the universal human feelings that are shared by the men and women of both the past and the present. But in order to be able to do so, we must fully understand the particular nature of the age in which the various classics were written.

THE AUTHOR OF THE TALE OF GENJI

NEMOTO: With that thought in mind, let us return to our discussion of the *Genji*. We should note at the outset that there are various theories concerning the authorship of the novel, or of parts of it. It is by no means certain that Lady Murasaki wrote the entire book. The famous woman poet Akiko Yosano (1878–1942), who made a modern-language translation of the *Genji,* has suggested that the chapters from "New Herbs" on are the work of Lady Murasaki's daughter, Daini no San'mi. It has also been suggested that the last ten chapters of the novel, known as the Uji chapters, are the work of some person or persons of a later period who lived in reclusion.

IKEDA: All are interesting theories. We must remember that in early times works of literature were not necessarily the products of single individuals. Many of them are more in the nature of joint undertakings carried out by several persons. And when we read the *Genji,* there are certain chapters that do indeed make us wonder if the work could be by a single writer.

NEMOTO: The three chapters immediately preceding the Uji chapters, particularly that entitled "Bamboo River," have often been regarded as the work of some other writer.

IKEDA: I would like to think, however, that Lady Murasaki is the author of most, if not all, of the novel. For one thing, that makes it easier for us to discuss it as a work of literature. At the same time, there is a uniform tone to the novel that runs throughout it and suggests a single author.

Lady Murasaki seems to have been a person of very meditative and introspective temperament. Reading her diary, the *Murasaki Shikibu nikki,* we notice that, while living as a lady-in-waiting amidst the splendor of the court, she often recorded her thoughts and reflections concerning her own way of life.

NEMOTO: Observing a water bird innocently enjoying itself on a pond, she composed the following sad poem:

> Water bird
> drifting on the surface,
> can I regard you with unconcern,
> when I too live
> in a world of drifting waters?

IKEDA: The poem perhaps expresses what may have been a fairly commonplace idea at the time. But in another place in her diary, Lady Murasaki, observing the palanquin bearers crouching down in order to maneuver a palanquin up a flight of steps, reflects upon her own position, remarking: "Are they any different from myself? Though we mingle with the great and mighty, each has his own position to fulfill, and I observe that none of us has an easy time of it." This suggests that she had a degree of sensitivity that was rather special for her time.

In "The Lady at the Bridge," the first of the ten Uji chapters, there is a passage in which the young nobleman Kaoru is pictured watching the rafts on the Uji River: "Strange, battered little boats, piled high with brush and wattles, made their way up and down the river, each boatman pursuing his own sad, small livelihood at the uncertain mercy of the waters. 'It is the same with all of us,' thought Kaoru to himself. 'Am I to boast that I am safe from the flood, calm and secure in a jeweled mansion?' "[1]

Here, I think, we see the same type of keen observation that is apparent in Lady Murasaki's diary. Reading such passages, I have the distinct impression that the Uji chapters, too, must be the work of Lady Murasaki herself.

NEMOTO: I can see what you mean. As has often been pointed out, the *Genji* is made up of three sections. The first section, which consists of the chapters up through that entitled "Wisteria Leaves," deals with Prince Genji's youth and his numerous love affairs. It was during this period that he built the magnificent new palace that we mentioned a bit earlier in our discussions. The second section, which begins with the two "New Herbs" chapters and ends with the chapter entitled "The Wizard," describes Genji's closing years. The last section, beginning with "His Perfumed Highness," deals with events after Genji's death and is in some sense a new story, though many of the characters are carried over from the earlier sections. The young nobleman Kaoru replaces Genji as the hero of these chapters. With the exception of the first three chapters in this section, all the other chapters—the so-called ten Uji chapters—center about the village of Uji some eleven miles south of the capital.

RESEMBLANCES TO TWENTIETH-CENTURY LITERATURE

IKEDA: It is a novel that covers a period of some seventy-five years, or three generations in the lives of its characters. Not to speak of its sheer bulk, it is a work whose scale of conception is all but unmatched in the history of Japanese literature.

NEMOTO: Through the English translation of Arthur Waley, it

has come to be numbered among the classics of world literature as a whole. The novelist and critic Masamune Hakuchō (1879–1962) said that it was only when he read the work in English translation that he realized how truly fascinating it was.

IKEDA: I myself have only read it all the way through in the modern Japanese language version by Jun'ichirō Tanizaki (1886–1965). I did, however, keep the original at my side and referred to it when I came to passages of particular interest. Sort of the opposite process from reading the original with a crib at hand.

Once I had the story as a whole in my head, I found that I could skip around here and there in the original and generally follow what I was reading. Parts that appealed to me, I went over very carefully. I admit it is a rather peculiar way of going about things—hardly what you would call the orthodox way of reading a classic of literature.

NEMOTO: On the contrary, it is a method that I would recommend to the average reader. After all, the language of the original is extremely difficult, and Japanese readers of today must have considerable training and practice before they can read the work accurately and with ease. And, as Shin'ichirō Nakamura has pointed out, novels must be read from beginning to end if one is to get a real sense of their flavor and charm.

In the West, the *Genji* has often been compared to Proust's *Remembrance of Things Past*. It would at first glance seem odd that an eleventh-century classic of Japanese literature should have anything in common with a highly innovative work of twentieth-century European literature.

IKEDA: The fact that the *Genji* has invited comparison with various works of modern literature is surely an indication of its depth and greatness. Its psychological descriptions have an astonishing subtlety that immediately suggests the techniques of the modern novel.

NEMOTO: Many critics have pointed out, however, that it lacks the tightness of construction that one usually finds in modern works of fiction of comparable length.

IKEDA: That is true. It would appear that Lady Murasaki did not start out with the intention of writing such a grandiose work. Most likely, as has been suggested, she at first thought only of producing a fairly brief romance for the amusement of the other women in the service of the court. But as she proceeded with her writing, the scope and outlook of her work gradually expanded and matured.

NEMOTO: The first section of the novel in some ways suggests a collection of short stories that are centered about certain re-curring characters. And they have about them the air of romance typical of earlier works of fiction such as *The Tale of the Bamboo Cutter* or the *Utsubo monogatari*. The impression is very different from that that one gets in reading the second and third sections, where the technique is one appropriate to a lengthy and sustained work of fiction.

IKEDA: In the first section, I believe the author was very much under the influence of the *Ise monogatari* (The Tales of Ise). Particularly in the earlier chapters, we find many accounts of passionate and often rather abandoned love affairs of youth that are quite similar in tone to those of *The Tales of Ise*.

NEMOTO: Yes—Prince Genji's romantic escapades. And yet they are not presented simply as a series of tales of amorous en-counters designed to titillate the reader. They are set against the background of the rivalry between Prince Genji's family and the powerful Fujiwara clan. While we read of the prince's romantic adventures, we also observe him ascending step by step to a position of political power. Thus there is an element of solid realism underlying the story.

IKEDA: In the chapter entitled "Fireflies" there occurs the

famous discussion of the art of fiction, in which the writer clearly reveals her artistic aspirations: ". . . They [works of fiction] have set down and preserved happenings from the age of the gods to our own. *The Chronicles of Japan* and the rest are a mere fragment of the whole truth. It is your romances that fill in the details." [2]

She is saying, in other words, that works of history are mere collections of facts. It is fiction alone that can show us the true nature of human beings. Thus, although Lady Murasaki was utilizing and carrying on the traditions of earlier Japanese romantic tales, her consciousness of the function and importance of fiction had already broken away from the stereotypes of the past. This came about because she was not content merely to examine the surface of reality but was by nature the type of person who probes deeply into the inner psychology of the self.

NEMOTO: This is what Motoori Norinaga, in his *Genji monogatari tama no ogushi,* meant when he singled out "the sensitivity to things" as the leading characteristic of the novel. His aim was to free the novel from approaches that would view it in the light of Buddhist or Confucian doctrine and to understand it as an attempt to deal with the subtleties of human emotion, to present a picture of human nature as it really is.

THE IDEOLOGICAL GROUNDWORK OF THE NOVEL

IKEDA: In view of the essential nature of literature, I would agree with that opinion. I believe it is a mistake to try to impose a didactic or ideological interpretation upon a work of literature. But, as I mentioned earlier, I have a feeling that the term "sensitivity to things" is likely to be taken in too emotional a sense. I would like to interpret it more as a subjective approach that, while coming fully to grips with the bitter realities of human life, attempts somehow to surmount them.

NEMOTO: That is the basic approach of Buddhism, or, rather, its point of departure.

IKEDA: Yes. And so I think we might say that Motoori, because of his antipathy toward Buddhism, somewhat misunderstood the true essence of the novel. It is an indication of the prejudices he held as an avid scholar and proponent of Japanese literature and culture. Of course, considering the corruption and arid dogmatism that characterized so much of the Buddhism of his time, it is not surprising that he should have had such prejudices.

NEMOTO: Motoori, while attempting to free the interpretation of the novel from the strictures of a fixed dogma, was at the same time to some extent restricted by his own ideological point of view.

IKEDA: As Motoori points out, it was certainly not Lady Murasaki's basic intention to use the novel to present an exposition of the doctrines of Tendai Buddhism. And yet to deny that there is any trace of Buddhist influence in the foundations of her thinking and sensitivity would, I believe, represent far too narrow a view of the matter.

NEMOTO: Yes, I agree.

IKEDA: Look at such Western writers as Dante, Milton or Victor Hugo. No one would deny, I think, that their works have their roots in Christian teachings. And yet they are not mere propaganda tracts for Christianity. Even Japanese who are not Christians and have no profound knowledge of Christianity are capable of being deeply moved when reading such works. This, needless to say, is because they deal with the universal truths of mankind.

I am not concerned here with any particular religious sect or system of dogma. And naturally I am not saying that it is impossible to have masterpieces of literature that are not founded upon some system of religious thought. But if we agree that literature is born from the very essentials of human existence, then I believe it is only proper that we should examine it in the light of religion and religious faith.

NEMOTO: Indeed, such an approach may be the key to a deeper and fuller understanding of works of literature.

IKEDA: For critics of the present age, who tend to deny the importance of religion or to look upon it lightly, Motoori Norinaga's interpretation of the *Genji* has proved an ideal weapon. And yet I wonder if they have not been too hasty and thoughtless in their acceptance of it.

Let me cite as an example a passage from the "Oak Tree" chapter. Prince Genji has just been informed that his wife has given birth to a son. The world supposes that it is his, but he knows that really the child was sired by the young nobleman Kashiwagi. He recalls with guilt how in his youth he carried on a secret affair with his father's mistress Fujitsubo and similarly sired a son that was believed to be his father's: "But how very strange it all was! Retribution had no doubt come for the deed which had terrified him then and which he was sure would go on terrifying him to the end. Since it had come, all unexpectedly, in this world, perhaps the punishment would be lighter in the next."[3]

It is possible to interpret the passage in a thoroughly modern manner, denying the doctrine of karmic retribution that underlies it and taking it simply as an example of the irony of fate. And even reading it in that fashion, we will be struck by its tone of verisimilitude. But if we do so, we will completely fail to comprehend the true nature of the feelings that troubled Prince Genji's soul.

NEMOTO: It is almost impossible to conceive of a system of ethics or morals that has no basis in religion and religious faith. Therefore, in order to understand the classics properly, it is not enough simply to take into consideration the political, economic, and social factors that influenced them. Only by analyzing them from the standpoint of religion and philosophy can we reach a deeper and more meaningful appreciation of them.

IKEDA: We often fail to see what is right in front of our eyes. Thus we find many Japanese stressing how important it is to have a knowledge of Christianity if one is to understand works of Western literature properly. And yet when it comes to the question of Buddhist influence in the classics of Japanese literature, in a surprising number of cases people are content simply to slide over the subject.

If we were to subtract the religious element from works of European fiction such as Tolstoy's *Resurrection* or Dostoevski's *Crime and Punishment,* they would become in effect merely popular novels of crime or blighted love, albeit very profound ones. And in the same way, it seems to me, if we subtract the element of religion from the *Genji,* it becomes no more than a novel of manners.

NEMOTO: It is not a question, of course, of whether or not the work of literature expounds any one particular system of religious thought.

IKEDA: No, certainly not. There is no need for the religious or ideological element to obtrude itself in a blatant manner in a work of literature. On the contrary, such elements should be thoroughly assimilated into the spirit of the writer himself.

The religious or ideological element constitutes the bone structure of the work of literature. But it must be judiciously fleshed out with literary expression if one is not to end up with a gaunt and ungainly creation.

THE DEPICTION OF THE TRANSIENCE OF LIFE

NEMOTO: On the other hand, if the literary expression is too elaborate and colorful and the bone structure weak, the work may appear overwrought and ineffectual. One will have sired not a skinny child, but a fat and overfed one.

IKEDA: Thought and expression, in other words, must be perfectly matched and fused. We have, for example, the concept of *mujō,* the transience or mutability of life, which we have already mentioned earlier. It may be said that the principal theme of the *Genji* is this concept of the transience of life, particularly human life. In the chapters entitled "The Law" and "The Mirage" in the second section of the novel, we find the earlier brilliance and glory that had characterized the world of Prince Genji giving way to a deep sense of decline and desolation. The poem by Prince Genji that closes the "Wizard" chapter conveys to the reader a vivid awareness of the inescapable evanescence of life:

> "I have not taken account of the days and months.
> The end of the year—the end of a life as well?" [4]

And even before this, the author has made the same point more subtly and at length by depicting the death of Murasaki, Prince Genji's companion from the years of his youth, and the lonely sorrowings of Prince Genji during the four seasons of the year following her death.

We should also keep in mind that it is because the opening section of the novel has so brilliantly described the youth and glory of Prince Genji that the second section, with its theme of the evanescence of such glory, can move us so profoundly.

NEMOTO: It has also been suggested that time itself is the principal theme of the *Genji.*

IKEDA: That strikes me as simply another, and perhaps more modern, way of describing the sense of transience that we have been discussing. The sense of transience is nothing other than a realistic recognition of the process of change inherent in all living beings as they exist in the dimension of time.

But at the root of this impermanence there is something

permanent. If we examine the nature of time carefully, we will find that it is nothing other than the moment by moment flaring of the life force. There is a firm and undeniable reality to the process. And the attempt to discover this abiding reality that exists within the phenomenon of impermanence is what gives rise to the emotion of *aware,* the sensitivity to life and the things about one that we talked about earlier.

NEMOTO: So you would not necessarily link up the awareness of the impermanence of life with the type of religious or philosophical resignation that is so often associated with it?

IKEDA: That is correct. In fact, however, the sense of impermanence or the transience of life as it is reflected in Heian literature contains a rather strong element of aesthetic consciousness. In a way, the concept of impermanence has become formalized and is treated almost as a decorative element. One might say it is a view of transience that has been adapted to the aristocratic tastes of the time.

NEMOTO: Buddhism itself was to some degree adapted to such tastes. The Buddhism of the aristocracy, of the mountain monastery or retreat, tends to be looked upon as a kind of refuge in which one can escape from the pain and vexations of daily life.

IKEDA: Yes. And that is one reason why the concept of the impermanence of life came to be associated with the idea of resignation or a kind of negative assent to the hopelessly fleeting quality of life.

True Buddhist understanding, of course, does not imply merely an attempt to escape or withdraw from life. On the contrary, it denotes a vigorous and forceful attitude and manner of life that is founded upon a frank recognition of the phenomenon of impermanence. Unfortunately, however, there is a tendency to interpret it in passive and contemplative terms alone.

THE TEN STATES OF EXISTENCE

NEMOTO: Generally speaking, any system of thought, if it is taken up with enthusiasm by the aristocracy, the priesthood, or the members of the intellectual class, is likely to be used at times for mere displays of erudition and refinement.

IKEDA: Buddhism speaks of the so-called ten states of existence. The first six of these, known as the Six Worlds, represent the basic elements of human life. In the course of daily life, the individual keeps passing from one to another of these six worlds or realms and experiencing the feelings of joy, anger, sorrow, or delight that pertain to them.

This, the reality of life, is looked upon as fundamentally impermanent and transient. And in contrast to the attitude that merely accepts and is content with this daily round of existence, Buddhism encourages an attitude that is more reflective, more critical in its consciousness of reality. This attitude is exemplified in the seventh and eighth of the ten states of existence, those of the *shōmon* and the *engaku*. These, in effect, represent the life of the intellectual. As such, they embody a certain degree of religious enlightenment. But it is an enlightenment that tends to be bound to the realm of conceptualization. It is likely to fall into a kind of aesthetic or philosophical intoxication, and, in the end, too often to seek only for self-fulfillment. In its attitude toward the realities of life, it lacks the dynamic willpower and regenerative force that should be a vital outcome of the recognition of impermanence.

NEMOTO: The religious faith and attitude of the characters of the *Genji* displays something of the tone of disillusionment and disgust with reality that you have suggested in your description of the seventh and eighth states of existence.

IKEDA: Generally speaking, the impulse to seek religious understanding and consolation appears most strongly at times when there has been some drastic disruption of the otherwise fairly stable conditions of life. At such times, the individual is led to question the premises upon which his or her existence is based, premises that had previously seemed firm and unshakable.

In Heian literature, this type of spiritual crisis tends to be treated in a rather stereotyped manner. This is in a sense an indication of the degree to which Buddhist concepts had become prevalent in the thinking of the time. But it can also be taken to indicate that the search for religious understanding or the retreat to the monastery or nunnery had come to be looked on as mere conventions or literary clichés.

NEMOTO: In the *Genji*, we find a number of the characters, such as Emperor Suzaku or the women Fujitsubo, Oborozukiyo, Utsusemi, Nyosan, and Ukifune, responding to such spiritual crisis by entering the Buddhist order to become monks or nuns. But all of them are pictured as taking this step in an attempt to extricate themselves from some difficult political position or an otherwise intolerable situation in their lives—in other words, to escape from reality.

IKEDA: In the case of the two heroes of the novel, Genji and Kaoru, however, the author does not permit them to retire from the world that easily. This fact, I believe, points up a very important feature in Lady Murasaki's thinking and outlook.

NEMOTO: In the case of Genji, although there are indications that he may be about to enter the priesthood, we never learn whether he in fact does so, since the narrative concerning his later years breaks off abruptly. The chapter entitled "Cloud Retreat" is said to have described the close of his life. But nothing remains of the chapter outside of the title, and it is not even certain whether it was ever written.

IKEDA: Personally I do not believe that it was.

NEMOTO: Kaoru, the hero of the latter portion of the novel, is only twenty-eight years old when the story comes to an end. Thus we do not know whether or not he ever retired from the world and became a monk. Of course, many people have suggested that the novel is unfinished.

IKEDA: When Lady Murasaki began the writing of the Uji chapters, I think she must already have had in mind carrying the story beyond the point at which it ends in its present version. I have a feeling she intended to involve Kaoru in a number of further cares and worldly entanglements. There are various hints in the extant sections that this was the direction the story would have taken if she had gone on with it.

As it is, however, the story breaks off before reaching its completion. Whether this is due to the death of the author or to some other cause, we do not know. And yet, to me at least, the present ending seems almost inevitable in terms of the nature of the story, a kind of resolution of the unresolved.

NEMOTO: Because of the fact that it does break off in this unresolved fashion, it has a kind of mysterious suggestiveness that it might otherwise not possess.

PROFILE OF THE RELIGIOUS MAN

IKEDA: This feature of the novel is related to the theme of the work as a whole, which we have identified as the sense of impermanence. But here I would like to consider for a time the way in which Prince Genji and Kaoru are portrayed.

Prince Genji, it seems to me, is pictured in three aspects: as a lover, as a wielder of political power, and as a man of religion. The first two aspects, as we have mentioned earlier, constitute the theme of the first section of the novel. In these chapters the prince, for all his amorous adventures, is not portrayed simply as a man for whom love is the sole aim and interest in life. He is depicted as a man of political concerns as well, taking part in what kind of complicated machinations we can only guess. This, it seems to me, is an indication of the acute social awareness of the author, who was not content to portray him in the fashion of the romantic heroes of earlier fiction.

NEMOTO: Lady Murasaki, as she mentions in her own diary, was nicknamed the Japanese Chronicle Lady because of her knowledge of Japanese works of history. It is obvious that she had an understanding of history that was quite unusual among the women writers of the time.

IKEDA: As a rule, in the works of fiction of the Heian period, the schemes and machinations that went on in the political sphere are never clearly depicted. Prince Genji's own political activities may have been too refined in manner to be called Machiavellian. And yet the political side of his life is portrayed in sufficient detail to lend an added dimension to his character as a whole.

NEMOTO: The depth and even deviousness of Prince Genji's character is brought out very strikingly in the banquet scene at which he and the young nobleman Kashiwagi find themselves face to face. Genji is aware that Kashiwagi has seduced his wife Nyosan and made her pregnant. While Kashiwagi suffers in silence over his guilty secret, Genji adopts a drunken and unknowing air, weeping in a maudlin manner with the other older men: " 'An old man does find it harder and harder to hold back drunken tears,' said Genji. He looked at Kashiwagi, 'And just see our young guardsman here, smiling a superior smile to make us feel uncomfortable. Well, he has only to wait a little longer. The current of the years runs only in one direction, and old age lies downstream.' " [5]

IKEDA: It is a very impressive scene. But what adds further depth to the portrayal of Genji's character is the depiction of the religious side of his nature. With this theme, the author turns directly to an examination of the basic problems of human suffering—the impermanence of life and the inevitability of death—issues that lie at the very heart of the novel.

NEMOTO: It is these issues that form the keynote of the second section of the work.

IKEDA: This is only an idea of mine. But I wonder if Lady Murasaki, in presenting her depiction of Genji as an ideal human being who possesses in full measure all the talents and beauties that could be desired, did not have in mind the so-called thirty-two distinguishing features and eighty physical characteristics that are said to adorn the body of the Buddha.

Prince Genji is, of course, consistently referred to as Hikaru Genji, the Shining Prince. This concept of a kind of brilliant light that emanates from the body of someone of great beauty or holiness seems to have entered Japan by way of the Buddhist scriptures, where it is associated with the figure of the Buddha. It has even been suggested that the depictions of Amaterasu were influenced by this concept.

Something like the same phenomenon may be seen in the depiction of Kaoru, the other hero of the novel, as well. In his case, however, it is not light but a mysterious fragrance that emanates from his body. In the "Eastern Cottage" chapter, the ladies-in-waiting remark upon this fragrance that lingers about him and compare it to the "perfume of Sandalwood of the Bull's Head Mountain," which, according to the "Yakuōbon," the twenty-third chapter of the *Lotus Sutra*, will issue from the mouth of the true believer.

NEMOTO: The implication, I suppose, is that such persons are reincarnations of some Buddha or Bodhisattva.

IKEDA: This implication is clear in the image of Genji, who, fulfilling the prophecies of the Korean and Japanese astrologers made when he was a child, in time attains the height of worldly glory. And the palace that he built, the Rokujō-in, was intended as a symbol of the re-creation upon earth of the Pure Land of the Buddha Amida.

In such passages we see the reflection of the actual political leaders of the time, such as Fujiwara no Michinaga—men who gave themselves up to the pleasure-filled life of the aristocracy but who, in order to allay the boundless feelings of anxiety that beset them, founded magnificent Buddhist temples such as the Hōjō-ji and the Byōdō-in.

But after these passages, the story develops in a new direction. The second section of the novel represents in a sense a criticism and negation of the first section, showing the antithesis upon which a new synthesis will be based. We are no longer dealing with a romantic tale in which reality is colored over with visionary longings for the transcendental world of Buddhist paradises. At the same time that the author impresses upon us the impermanence of worldly glory, she confronts Genji, who has now passed beyond the phase of amorous adventures and political ambitions, with a far more difficult problem. It is the problem of human salvation itself, of how one should live with the impermanence of reality and in time win out over it.

NEMOTO: And thus Genji, the seeker of Truth, the religious man, is born.

IKEDA: Yes. But, as the author no doubt realized, there are limits to the degree that the character of Prince Genji as it exists within the world of the novel can be extended and developed. Thus Lady Murasaki abandons him and introduces a new hero, Kaoru, in the third section of the work. Through the figure of Kaoru she is able to deal in a new setting with the problems that confronted Genji in the course of his lifetime. Kaoru is not related to Genji by blood. But spiritually, I believe, we should look upon him as Genji's heir.

A CREATIVE VIEW OF THE INDIVIDUAL

NEMOTO: That is an interesting point. In that case the last section of the book is linked in theme with the sections that precede it. And yet, as we have noted earlier, whatever Lady Murasaki may have been attempting to achieve in it, the last section of the work in its present state is unresolved.

IKEDA: That, I would say, is no more than a formal limitation in the work. The function of literature is not to solve problems but is to present an attempt at a solution, or simply to set forth the problem itself. Thus the fact that the last section of the novel was written at all is of primary importance. In terms of literary appeal, however, it may seem to lack the liveliness and variety that characterize the earlier sections of the work.

NEMOTO: You are suggesting, then, that the last section is of interest mainly because of its thought content?

IKEDA: When we speak of thought content, we should not imagine anything like the penetrating speculation or profound philosophical debate so often found in works of Western fiction. And yet there are qualities about Kaoru—his melancholy brooding, his nagging doubts about his parentage—that remind one of the philosophically minded heroes of Western fiction, such as Faust. We will recall that Kaoru, though believed by the world to be the son of Genji, was really the son of the nobleman Kashiwagi, who had seduced Genji's wife Nyosan. Thus, in the "His Perfumed Highness" chapter, we read of him: "He could only brood in solitude and ask what missteps in a former life might explain the painful doubts with which he had grown up—and wish that he had the clairvoyance of a Prince Rāhula, who instinctively knew the truth about his own birth.

"Whom might I ask? Why must it be
That I do not know the beginning or the end?"[6]

Of course, Kaoru's way of life has none of the forceful and positive nature of that of Faust, who actively sought to taste to the full all the experiences of human life and dreamed of the time when he might gain perfect knowledge:

> Then shall I see, with vision clear,
> How secret elements cohere,
> And what the universe engirds,
> And give up huckstering with words. [7]

Kaoru's search for knowledge and religious Truth remains always within the world of emotion and sentiment. In comparison to Faust, his attitude is one of passivity and resignation.

NEMOTO: Which reflects the religious consciousness of the society in which Kaoru—or rather the writer of the novel—lived.

IKEDA: Yes. Even Lady Murasaki could not free herself from the social and ideological conditions imposed upon her by the period. And yet, through her presentation of Genji and Kaoru as men of religious concerns, she was able to add a greater depth to the world depicted in the *Genji* and to grapple with the eternal problems of human destiny. And it is important to note that she did not present the concerns of love, politics, and religion as entirely disparate elements within the makeup of her characters but rather as concentric circles contained one within another. This is an indication of the unique creativity with which she apprehended the human personality.

❖ ❖ ❖ ❖ ❖ ❖ ❖ ❖ ❖ ❖ ❖ ❖ ❖ ❖ ❖

6. *The Tale of Genji* and the *Lotus Sutra*

❖ ❖ ❖ ❖ ❖ ❖ ❖ ❖ ❖ ❖ ❖ ❖ ❖ ❖ ❖

THE "CONSCIOUSNESS-ONLY" ANALYSIS OF THE HUMAN BEING

NEMOTO: In the previous discussion we talked about the way and manner in which Lady Murasaki portrayed the character of Genji and pointed out the creativity with which she apprehended the human personality. I wonder if we could pursue that point a little further.

IKEDA: In comparison with the older romances that preceded it in Japanese literature, the *Genji* presents a very new and in some ways modern understanding of the human being. The outstanding feature of it is that it does not view the character of the individual as one-sided or fixed in nature.

NEMOTO: As we have noted earlier, this manner of perception probably owes much to the deeply reflective nature of the author herself.

IKEDA: I surely think so. And at the same time I believe that it reflects a strong Buddhist influence. There are elements in it that suggest various Buddhist philosophies such as that known as *Yuishiki,* or Consciousness-Only.

NEMOTO: That is one of the basic schools of Buddhist philosophy. In this system, the five senses are designated as the five consciousnesses. To these it adds a sixth, the sense-center consciousness; a seventh, the mind consciousness; and an eighth, the *ālaya* consciousness. This last is an underlying store of perceptions that lies deep within the individual and, when influenced by the "seeds," or effects of good and evil deeds, produces the phenomena of the external world.

IKEDA: The doctrine is an attempt to probe deep within the unconsciousness of the individual and to discover some fundamental reality that is untouched by the concepts of good and evil. The Tendai school of Buddhism goes even further in postulating a ninth consciousness, the *kompon-jōshiki,* or fundamental pure consciousness.

We need not go into these complex and difficult doctrines here. But we should note that Lady Murasaki undoubtedly had some degree of knowledge concerning them. How far she had actually studied them, I do not know, but she seems to have had some kind of intuitive grasp of their nature and implications.

NEMOTO: By her time, Buddhist ways of thought had already penetrated deeply into Japanese life as a whole.

IKEDA: Yes. They had been absorbed to a considerable degree.

NEMOTO: In this connection, I wonder how we ought to view the frequent mentions of malicious or vengeful spirits that occur in the *Genji*. The tale of how the jealous spirit of Lady Rokujō takes possession of and eventually kills Genji's first wife, Aoi, though we may wish to dismiss it as a mere ghost story, is presented with an uncanny air of realism.

IKEDA: First of all, I wonder if such beliefs were not influenced by the manner of life that prevailed among the people of the time. The interiors of the rooms in which they lived were dark to a degree that it is almost impossible for us today to imagine. Only when there is a power failure do we have any inkling of what the situation was like. Unless we consider how it must have been to live in such dark rooms, the occupants further hidden behind blinds and curtains of state, with only a flickering torch to provide illumination, I do not think we can comprehend the feeling of terror that is expressed through such tales.

NEMOTO: It is not surprising that the people of the Heian period should have had such a profound belief in the existence of evil spirits.

IKEDA: I suppose we could say it was a mere superstition and dismiss it with a laugh. But I do not think that Lady Murasaki looked at it that way.

We could perhaps interpret the account of Aoi's possession as revealing a strain of jealousy and malice that existed within the unconscious of Lady Rokujō. But it is important to note that it is Genji, and not the others around Aoi, who perceives the evil spirit to be that of Lady Rokujō. I would like to speculate that, rather than being an emanation of Lady Rokujō, the "evil spirit" may in fact be a manifestation of something hidden away deep within the psychology of Genji himself. I have a strong feeling that it is a materialization of an alter ego or abiding sense of guilt that Genji himself is not aware exists within him.

NEMOTO: That is a very interesting observation. And I suppose it would tie in with what we have said earlier about the ālaya consciousness in our remarks on the Consciousness-Only school of philosophy.

IKEDA: There is perhaps no direct connection between the two. And yet I think we can say that Lady Murasaki's acute powers of observation often find expression in ways that fit in with the analysis of the human personality set forth in the Consciousness-Only doctrines.

CHANGES IN THE RELIGIOUS OUTLOOK OF THE TIME

NEMOTO: I would like to consider in further detail just what kind of Buddhist thought is reflected in the *Genji*. By the time the novel was written, some four or five hundred years had passed since the introduction of Buddhism to Japan. During that period, Japanese Buddhism had undergone various changes.

I wonder to what degree we can discern the influence of the *Lotus Sutra* in the novel? Heian-period Buddhism, of course, was dominated by two principal sects: the Tendai sect, introduced to Japan by Saichō (767–822), and the Shingon sect, introduced by Kūkai (774–835). In the *Genji*, we find mention of evil spirits, as we have noted, and descriptions of prayers and incantations carried out in an attempt to save persons who are ill or dying, a practice particularly associated with Shingon, or Esoteric Buddhism. In addition, there are many evidences of the belief in the Western Paradise of the Buddha Amida into which believers are reborn after death.

IKEDA: Yes, there are certainly elements of Esoteric Buddhism and Amidist beliefs in the novel. Tendai Buddhism, which was centered at Mount Hiei, close to the capital, had already become fused with such elements by the time Lady Murasaki was writing. And new tendencies were also developing within the Tendai sect.

NEMOTO: The new type of Tendai Buddhism that developed out of the fusion of these elements came to be known as Tendai Esotericism, in contrast to the older Shingon Esotericism introduced by Kūkai. It was already beginning to take shape by the time of the third head of the Tendai sect, Jigaku Ennin (794–864).

IKEDA: Yes.

NEMOTO: The Amidist, or Pure Land, doctrines seem to have appeared in Tendai Buddhism around the middle of the tenth century and became extremely popular in the following period, when the Fujiwara family was at the height of its power. During the eleventh century, when the Fujiwaras exercised power as regents or when the retired emperors were in control of the government, Amidist beliefs enjoyed their greatest vogue among the society of the Heian aristocrats.

IKEDA: One of the leading exponents of Pure Land thought was Genshin (942–1017), a Tendai monk who wrote a work entitled the *Ōjōyōshū* (Essentials of Salvation). He is said to have been the model for the monk known as the Sōzu of Yokawa who appears in the final chapters of the *Genji.*

NEMOTO: This form of Buddhism seems to have exercised very little influence during the Nara and early Heian periods, when the bureaucratic system of government was still functioning effectively. According to Mitsusada Inoue, this was because the Amidist teachings tended to look upon the present world as a realm of defilement, in contrast to the Pure Land of the Buddha Amida. Such a view did not appeal to the intellectuals of the bureaucratic period, who were then enjoying considerable power and affluence.

Later, however, when the Fujiwara clan gradually usurped the power of government and forced the other members of the intellectual class into the shade, Amidism began to enjoy increasing popularity, providing spiritual solace to those whose worldly fortunes had declined. It is ironic that it was also taken up with enthusiasm by the Fujiwaras themselves. For men such as Fujiwara no Michinaga, who enjoyed positions of the highest power, it constituted the mainstay of their spiritual and religious life.

IKEDA: It has been suggested that the three large sections of the

Genji reflect, though perhaps only inadvertently, the changing religious consciousness of the time. Professor Hōun Iwase, in his book *Genji monogatari to Bukkyō shisō* (*The Tale of Genji* and Buddhist Thought), has offered substantial proof to support this idea. He begins by pointing out that though Tendai Buddhism centers about the doctrine of the One Vehicle of the true Mahayana as expounded in the *Lotus Sutra,* it also embraced Esoteric and Amidist elements. As time passed, however, the focus came to be more upon the Amidist doctrines.

NEMOTO: It is certain that Amidist thinking is strongly reflected in the Uji chapters of the *Genji,* which express a feeling of pessimism and turning away from the world.

IKEDA: Iwase has made a careful study of various terms that express an attitude of affirmation or denial toward the world as they occur in the *Genji.* He points out that the term *gan,* which designates a religious vow taken in the hope of gaining some particular end and exemplifies the Esoteric attitude of affirmation of the present world, appears most often in the first section of the novel. It is on the contrary used very seldom in the last section and never in connection with the hero Kaoru.

The term *tsune nashi,* or impermanence, which suggests a motive for turning away from the world, is found throughout the work but is especially frequent in passages dealing with Genji and Kaoru. Terms that go a step further and brand the world as a realm of defilement from which one withdraws in disgust, however, are found only in the last section.

NEMOTO: That is an extremely interesting analysis.

IKEDA: I do not think that Lady Murasaki consciously planned that the novel should develop in this fashion. Rather, I believe we have here a reflection of an almost inevitable spiritual process by which she moved from a naive affirmation of reality to an increasing awareness of the transience of life and then sought some means by which to conquer or resolve the dilemma that resulted.

Lady Murasaki was no doubt influenced by the Amidist ideas and attitudes that were so prevalent in her time. But, at least within the fictional realm of her novel, she did not give in to any easy pessimism or attitude of withdrawal from the world. On the contrary, to the end she kept her eyes fixed upon the sufferings and anomalies of reality.

LADY MURASAKI'S VIEW OF BUDDHISM

NEMOTO: In a sense, the theme that runs through the entire novel is the investigation of the phenomenon of impermanence.

IKEDA: And in relation to this central literary theme the elements of Esoteric and Amidist Buddhism are no more than ornamentations to the world of the novel, not forces that lend it positive support.

NEMOTO: You would see the philosophy of the *Lotus Sutra*, then, as the basis of her Buddhism?.

IKEDA: Yes. I believe the influence of the *Lotus Sutra* as it was expounded in Tendai Buddhism constitutes the element of prime importance.

If we turn to the *Genji monogatari jiten* (*The Tale of Genji Encyclopedia*), compiled by Kikan Ikeda, we see at a glance exactly what Buddhist writings Lady Murasaki quotes or alludes to in her work. We note that she quotes rather frequently from Amidist texts such as the *Kammuryōju-kyō*, the *Amida-kyō*, and the *Essentials of Salvation* already mentioned. But by far the largest number of references are to the *Lotus Sutra*, along with the *Fugen-kyō* and the *Daihatsunehan-kyō* (Nirvana Sutra). Let me quote a few examples of the influence of the *Lotus Sutra*. In the chapter entitled "A Rack of Cloud," the death of Fujitsubo is described in these words: "And as he spoke she died, like a dying flame." [1] The description is based upon the lines in the first chapter of the *Lotus Sutra* that read:

> The Buddha passed away in that night
> As a fire dies out when the wood is gone.

Again, in the "Lavender" chapter, Genji says: "The guiding hand of the Blessed One makes no mistakes on the darkest nights." [2] This appears to be a recasting of the lines in the seventh chapter of the *Lotus Sutra* that read: "They go out of darkness into darkness, and never hear the names of the Buddhas."

NEMOTO: In the "Trefoil Knots" chapter, Kaoru refers to a story that is found in the *Nirvana Sutra:*

> "Deep in the Snowy Mountains would I vanish,
> In search of the brew that is death for those who love.

"If, like the lad of the Snowy Mountains, he had an accommodating monster of whom he might inquire about a stanza, he would have an excuse to fling himself away. A less than perfectly enlightened heart our young sage had!" [3]

IKEDA: And the same chapter contains an allusion to the Jōfukyō Bosatsu, the Never-Despising Bodhisattva, who is described in chapter twenty of the *Lotus Sutra*.

In the chapter entitled "At Writing Practice," the monk known as the Sōzu of Yokawa, whom we have mentioned earlier, says of Ukifune, whose origins are unknown to him: "If she is what she appears to be, a girl of good family, then the secret cannot be kept forever. Not of course that I would wish to be understood as saying that there are no beauties among girls of the lower classes. Ours is a world in which even the ogre maiden finds salvation.'" [4] This of course, is a reference to the famous story of the dragon king's daughter in chapter twelve of the *Lotus*

Sutra, who, despite the fact that she had been born as a lowly creature, attained Buddhahood. Right after the above quotation we find a reference to the belief, expounded in chapter eighteen of the *Lotus Sutra,* that virtue in a previous existence will lead one to be reborn with great natural beauty.

LADY MURASAKI'S DEVOTION TO THE LOTUS SUTRA

NEMOTO: Lady Murasaki seems to have been a rather devoted reader of the scriptures.

IKEDA: Yes, I think she was. Commentaries on the *Genji,* such as the *Kachō yojō* by Ichijō Kanera (1402–81) and the *Kogetsushō* by Kitamura Kigin (1624–1705), offer very detailed and interesting discussions of the influence of Buddhist scriptures upon the novel. They point out, for example, that the famous Gradations of Beauty passage in the second chapter of the novel, in which Genji and his male friends discuss various types of women, borrows its form from the so-called three stages of preaching in the *Lotus Sutra.*

NEMOTO: What exactly are the three stages of preaching?

IKEDA: In the second chapter of the *Lotus Sutra,* entitled "Expedients," Shākyamuni preaches the doctrine of *shohō-jissō,* which teaches that the variety of phenomenal things expresses the real state of the universal and eternal truth. But of all his disciples, only Shāriputra, who had a superior capacity for understanding such tenets, was able to gain enlightenment. This method of expanding the doctrine is known as *hossetsu-shū,* or preaching by theory.

Then, for the sake of his other disciples, Shākyamuni next preached the parables of the three types of carts and of the burning house, which are found in chapter three, "A Parable." As a result, the leading disciples Subhūti, Kātāyana, Kāshyapa, and Maudgalyāyana understood and gained enlightenment. This is known as *yusetsu-shū*, or preaching by parable.

Finally, for the sake of disciples of lesser capacity, such as Pūrna, who still did not understand, he preached the doctrine of causes from former lives, relating stories of the lives of past Buddhas. This is known as *innen-shū*, or preaching by causes, and is illustrated in chapter six of the *Lotus Sutra*.

The Gradations of Beauty passage in the *Genji*, we will notice, begins with observations on women in general. It then moves to a description of various hypothetical types of women, which correspond to the parables of the sutra. Finally it ends with the young men relating their own personal experiences with women, corresponding to the stories of former lives in the sutra. Thus, we are told, the whole passage is modeled upon the three types of preaching exemplified in the *Lotus Sutra*.

NEMOTO: That's all very interesting. But don't you think it was rather improper of Lady Murasaki to borrow the device for a discussion of women?

IKEDA: Oh, I don't think it was all that wicked a thing to do. In any event, the examples we have talked about so far are all related to the form or manner of expression of the novel. It is clear from other works, such as the *Pillow Book* of Sei Shōnagon, that the *Lotus Sutra* was commonly looked upon by the educated persons of the time as among the finest of the Buddhist scriptures. It is, therefore, not at all surprising to find it so often quoted or alluded to in the *Genji*.

NEMOTO: Nowadays even well-educated people are often quite ignorant of Buddhism. The people of the Heian period would probably be downright shocked at how little many modern Japanese know about the subject.

IKEDA: We have spoken earlier about Buddhist influence in the *Kojiki*. In the case of the *Genji*, of course, the influence is naturally far deeper and more pronounced. In the *Kojiki*, what influence there is seems to be confined mainly to matters of diction and mode of literary expression. With the *Genji*, however, the influence clearly penetrates far more deeply, affecting the content and thought of the work.

NEMOTO: In other words, it is intimately related to the theme of the novel as a whole—is that correct?

IKEDA: Yes. When discussing the thought content of the *Genji*, it is absolutely impossible to overlook the influence of Buddhist philosophy, particularly as it is expressed in the *Lotus Sutra*.

Buddhism begins by addressing itself to the problems of human life—those of birth, old age, sickness, and death. Approaching the question from various angles, it attempts to explain these phenomena and to point out some way to overcome them, to rescue the individual from them. What it offers in the end is an understanding of the ultimate nature of life itself. The Tendai doctrine of *ichinen sanzen,* or three thousand worlds in one instant of life, represents the crystallization of Buddhist thought as it is expounded in the *Lotus Sutra*.

Literature, we may say, is an attempt to discover the eternal and ultimate reality of life by confronting the phenomena that are involved in daily human existence. In terms of the ten states of existence, it is an attempt to press forward from the ninth state of existence to an understanding of the highest state, that of Buddhahood. In terms of the nine types of consciousness, it is an attempt to move from the sixth or seventh type of consciousness to the ninth.

NEMOTO: How, then, would you define the basic philosophy of the *Genji?*

IKEDA: I think we find it spelled out clearly in the famous passage in the "Fireflies" chapter that deals with the art of fiction. This is not only a discussion of the essential nature of fiction but at the same time is, I believe, a revelation of the principal theme that guided Lady Murasaki in the writing of her work. Thus she writes: ". . . If the storyteller wishes to speak well, then he chooses the good things; and if he wishes to hold the reader's attention he chooses bad things, extraordinarily bad things. Good things and bad things alike, they are things of this world and no other. . . . But to dismiss them as lies is itself to depart from the truth. Even in the writ which the Buddha drew from his noble heart are parables, devices for pointing obliquely at the truth. To the ignorant they may seem to operate at cross purposes. The Greater Vehicle is full of them, but the general burden is always the same. The difference between enlightenment and confusion is of about the same order as the difference between the good and the bad in a romance. If one takes the generous view, then nothing is empty and useless."[5]

In other words, though Lady Murasaki seems merely to be talking about the art of fiction, she is really dealing clearly with the problems of delusion and human life and death.

THE WORLD OF GENJI AND KAORU

NEMOTO: And the lives of Genji and Kaoru as they are depicted in the novel, I suppose, are related to these fundamental philosophical problems.

IKEDA: I believe that Lady Murasaki viewed all the sufferings and entanglements of daily existence as a kind of ladder by means of which one ascends to the ultimate enlightenment. In the chapter entitled "The Rites," Genji, plunged into grief by the death of his beloved companion, called Murasaki in the novel, reviews the course of his own life and reflects: "He thought back over his life. Even the face he saw in the mirror had seemed to single him out for unusual honors, but there had very early been signs that the Blessed One meant him more than others to know the sadness and evanescence of things. He had made his way ahead in the world as if he had not learned the lesson. And now had come grief which surely did single him out from all men, past and future." [6]

Again, in the chapter called "The Wizard," we find Genji speaking to his serving women in these words: " 'I have always had everything,' he said to them. 'That was the station in life I was born to. Yet it has always seemed that I was meant for sad things too. I have often wondered whether the Blessed One was not determined to make me see more than others what a useless, insubstantial world it is.' " [7]

NEMOTO: Kaoru comes to much the very same realization. Thus in the "Trefoil Knots" chapter, as he looks upon the dead form of Lady Oigimi, he remarks: "He wanted to find a flaw, something to make her seem merely ordinary. If the Blessed One meant by all this to bring renunciation and resignation, then let him present something repellent, to drive away the regrets." [8]

And again in the "Drake Fly" chapter, when Kaoru learns of the supposed death of Ukifune, he ponders despondently: "What a fleeting affair it had been! The pretty face, those winning ways, were gone forever. Why had he been so slow to act while she was alive, why had he not pressed his cause more aggressively? Numberless regrets burned within him, so intense that there was no quenching them. For him, at least, love seemed to be unrelieved torment. Perhaps the powers above were angry that, against his own better impulses, he had remained in the vulgar world. They had a way [*hōben*] of hiding their mercy, of subjecting a man to the sorest trials and imposing enlightenment upon him." [9]

IKEDA: Lady Murasaki's aim seems to have been to depict her heroes Genji and Kaoru as spending all their lives adrift upon the sea of human delusion and change, and yet as forever seeking for enlightenment and peace. They are portrayed as individuals who fluctuate constantly between the desire for religious truth and the entanglements of romantic passion.

Lady Murasaki herself appears to have been acutely conscious of human fate or karma, the fate imposed upon one by actions in a previous existence. No matter what amount of fancy and imagination may go into the composition of a work of literature, in the end it reflects the identity of the writer himself. And if we recognize this fact, then I think we must see the figures of Genji and Kaoru as in a sense embodiments of Lady Murasaki's own mental torments and anxieties.

NEMOTO: In several of these passages quoted from the *Genji*, we encounter the word hōben, or *upāya*.

IKEDA: Yes. It is probably derived from the second chapter of the *Lotus Sutra*, the "Hōben-bon" (Expedients) chapter. Nowadays one often hears people remark that "even lies are a kind of expedient," though that is rather too self-serving an interpretation of the word.

In Tendai philosophy, the word is interpreted in three ways, but I do not think we need to go into such technicalities here. Ordinarily it is taken to mean the various expedient means adopted, according to the circumstances and the capacities of the hearers, to lead ordinary beings to an understanding of the highest truths.

Thus, in terms of the *sanjō*, or three kinds of teaching given by the Buddha, those who are in the realm of the *shrāvaka* are taught to understand the Four Noble Truths; those in the realm of the *pratyeka* are taught to understand the twelvefold chain of causation; and those in the realm of the Bodhisattva are taught to observe the six *pāramitās*. But all of these are hōben, or expedient means designed to lead one to the truth of the One Vehicle of Mahayana Buddhism.

But as made clear in the "Expedients" chapter of the *Lotus Sutra*, the three vehicles are actually identical with the One Vehicle. Thus the chapter states: "These Buddhas employ countless and innumerable expedients, various tales of karma, parables, and discourses to expound the doctrines for the benefit of all beings. And these doctrines are all expounded for the sake of the One Buddha Vehicle." We have already noted above how Lady Murasaki, in her discussion of fiction, makes use of the same concept of hōben.

We find the word hōben used again in the "Juryō-bon," chapter sixteen of the *Lotus Sutra*. There it appears in the famous parable of the good physician who resorted to a trick in order to make his sons, who had drunk poison and lost their minds, drink the medicine he had prepared for them. As the physician says: "Now I will make use of an expedient to persuade them to take the medicine." In this parable the sons stand for all sentient beings and the physician for the Buddha. As the verse section of the chapter states: "It is like the physician who used a good expedient to cure his mad sons."

Hōun Iwase, drawing his evidence from such commentaries on the *Genji* as the *Kachō yojō* and the *Kogetsushō*, expounds at great length the view that the sufferings that Genji and Kaoru are called upon to endure in life are in fact hōben. I believe we would be justified in saying that the theory of the use of expedient means as it is expounded in the sutras has exerted a definite influence on the novel.

NEMOTO: It would certainly seem to have done so.

IKEDA: This type of interpretation, however, would probably be rejected by Motoori Norinaga.

THE RELATIONSHIP BETWEEN DELUSION AND ENLIGHTENMENT

NEMOTO: I guess we will just have to risk his disapproval. But I would like to inquire a little more about the relationship between delusion and enlightenment.

The word *bonnō*, or delusion, is usually taken to refer to the "three poisons" of greed, anger, and ignorance and to the other sufferings and afflictions of human life, while *bodai*, or enlightenment, refers to a state of understanding and happiness. It is generally supposed that the object of Buddhist practice is to free oneself from delusions and to attain enlightenment.

In the *Lotus Sutra,* with its doctrine of the ten states of existence all contained within one another, we find that delusions and enlightenment are, in fact, inseparable. The principle is summed up in the phrase *bonnō-soku-bodai.* In other words, there is no cutting off of delusion.

IKEDA: That is right.

NEMOTO: In that case, then, the state of delusion just as it exists constitutes the state of enlightenment.

IKEDA: That is not quite correct. If we accept such a view, then we are likely to make the error of approving of delusions as they exist. This will lead us back into an uncritical and facile affirmation of reality. Originally, delusion and enlightenment were regarded as strictly opposite and opposing concepts. The view expressed by the phrase bonnō-soku-bodai, which seems to ignore this opposition, cannot be taken either as a simple affirmation of reality or as an attempt to flee from reality.

NEMOTO: The same opposition may be seen in the consciousness of the aristocrats of the Heian period. On the one hand, they prized worldly glory above all else, while on the other, they expressed a weariness with the world and a desire to escape from it.

IKEDA: Such opposing tendencies are often to be found in society. But the key to the understanding of the phrase bonno-soku-bodai lies in the word soku, a word of very profound and suggestive meaning. We should be careful not to interpret it in too simple or superficial a manner.

NEMOTO: There is certainly a distinct danger of that.

IKEDA: Soku represents a relationship between two entities—

"non-dual" or "inseparable." In modern terms I see it as the resolution of contradictions, the principle of sublation, or particularly as the principle of change and practice.

To produce enlightenment out of delusion is a very drastic leap forward. What makes it possible is the power of the Buddha and the Dharma—that is, the merit bestowed by the Buddhist teachings themselves. On the other hand, there must also be the power of belief and practice involved—that is, the subjective religious practices of the believer himself. In other words, I would like to see soku, which transforms delusion into enlightenment, as containing within it the powerful spring of faith and practice.

Reality confronts us with various kinds of suffering and anomaly. We must not try to run away from reality. And neither must we compromise with it, resign ourselves, and sink into slumber. Rather we must, while always keeping our gaze fixed steadily upon it, work untiringly to change it. Then the highest type of enlightenment can be created out of delusion and suffering, and a new and elevated flow of life will make its appearance.

NEMOTO: In other words, it is not something to be achieved simply by meditation or contemplation.

IKEDA: Surely no. Lady Murasaki, while realizing the difficulty of crossing over from delusion to enlightenment, probably glimpsed where the solution lay. It appears to have been almost a convention among the aristocrats of the Heian period to profess a desire to withdraw from the world and enter the Buddhist clergy. If one were to speak in harsh terms, they seem to have hoped thereby to obtain pardon for their sins and entrance into the Pure Land. And for that reason Lady Murasaki seems on the contrary to have taken a rather critical attitude toward such professions. No doubt she was also thoroughly familiar with the type of monks who served the men in worldly power, monks who knew only the provisional teachings.

NEMOTO: A religion that enters into cohesion with worldly authority is bound to lose the power to carry out its basic mission.

IKEDA: Yes. I believe so. And the source of Genji's and Kaoru's sorrow lay in the fact that, while aware of their own profound ignorance and delusion and believing in the possibility of some kind of basic salvation, they were unable to discover any force or means that they might rely upon in seeking it. Thus Genji, in the chapter entitled "The Wizard," looking at the letters left behind by Murasaki after her death, composes a poem that reads:

> "I seek to follow the tracks of a lady now gone
> To another world. Alas, I lose my way." [10]

And Kaoru, in "The Floating Bridge of Dreams," the last chapter in the novel, sends the following poem to Ukifune:

> "I lost my way in the hills, having taken a road
> That would lead, I hope, to a teacher of the Law." [11]

Both poems, I believe, echo the inner sentiments of the author of the *Genji* herself.

In my remarks on the novel, it is possible that I have placed too much emphasis upon the Buddhist element. The *Genji* must, of course, always be read as a work of literature composed by a single individual. And yet I think there can be no doubt that its greatness as a work of literature and its appeal to readers throughout the world derive primarily from the deep religious and philosophical foundations that underlie the novel. In considering the direction taken by most of our present-day works of literature, it would be useful to keep that fact in mind.

❖ PART FOUR ❖

The World of
the *Konjaku Monogatari*

❖ ❖ ❖ ❖ ❖ ❖ ❖ ❖ ❖ ❖ ❖ ❖ ❖ ❖ ❖

7. Man in an Age of Transition

❖ ❖ ❖ ❖ ❖ ❖ ❖ ❖ ❖ ❖ ❖ ❖ ❖ ❖

A PERIOD OF EPOCHAL CHANGE

NEMOTO: I understand you have just returned from a forty-day trip to North and South America. You must be tired!

IKEDA: No. As you can see, I'm as lively as ever. I guess that meeting and talking with so many busy and energetic friends abroad gives me a new charge of energy.

NEMOTO: I understand the interest in the occult continues as before in the United States. We are even beginning to feel the effects of it over here. Books on Esoteric Buddhism and discussions on psychic powers are enjoying a great vogue. At the same time, there seems to have been a growing interest in Buddhism and Buddhist texts in general over the past few years. What do you think of these trends?

IKEDA: Exorcisms and all that? If we examine the various fads and interests closely, we find many that are odd and even contradictory. Perhaps they do not even represent a single trend in people's thinking. And yet, if we take a larger view, we can perhaps say that they reflect an overall tendency in the world today.

NEMOTO: It is often remarked that the present interest in Asian thought and philosophy, and in Buddhism in particular, results from a kind of disillusionment with modern rational ways of thought.

IKEDA: There is certainly that element to it. In the past few centuries human civilization has made astounding progress in many fields, and the enrichment in our material lives has been truly impressive. But at the same time problems relating to man's spiritual life have tended to be neglected. So we have what might be called a sense of spiritual hunger and dissatisfaction. And at the same time the material benefits that have resulted from this recent progress are very unequally distributed among mankind as a whole, resulting in a dramatic lack of balance between the so-called haves and the have-nots. What is more, modern civilization itself, with its constant and imperative search for progress and material richness, has begun to display elements within itself that could very well bring about its own destruction.

NEMOTO: The problems of warfare and environmental pollution have led men to question the whole manner and direction of modern civilization.

IKEDA: Yes. During my latest trip to America, I felt this very strongly. Just how far it is a conscious movement at this point is difficult to say. But I think there is a growing awareness that such problems are common to all mankind and can be solved only through the cooperation of all. In that sense, our present twentieth century may turn out to be one of epochal change.

NEMOTO: The values that have dominated the postwar world and, in a larger sense, the world of the twentieth century as a whole up to the present moment are being called into question. There is an intense searching about for new values and goals, which is surely one of the marks of an age of transition.

IKEDA: I would like to see the growing interest in Buddhism that you mention as a phenomenon connected with, and perhaps even brought about by, this search for new values, for some key that will open the doors to a new era.

On earlier occasions I have spoken rather sweepingly of the twenty-first century as the "Human Century" or the "Century of the Life Force." I used such terms because I have a distinct feeling that we are witnessing a kind of universal upsurge of human hopes and aspirations.

NEMOTO: In our next discussions we will be talking about the *Konjaku monogatari,* a collection of popular tales, many of them Buddhist in nature, that was probably compiled in the twelfth century, at the close of the Heian period. In terms of Japanese history, this, too, was an age of dramatic change and transition. In our discussions, I hope we can consider the ways in which the problems of that age may relate to those of our own time.

A WORLD FREED FROM OPPRESSION

IKEDA: In its present form, the *Konjaku* consists of twenty-eight chapters and contains tales from India and China, as well as those that originated in Japan. The amount of material is staggering, and I confess I have only read here and there in the work in the parts that caught my interest. But even in a partial reading, I was struck by a feeling of freshness in the content and outlook of the work.

The earlier works of Japanese literature that we have been

discussing, such as the *Kojiki* and the *Genji* (and even the *Man'yōshū*, though it is somewhat different in nature), were all produced at a time when the Fujiwara clan dominated the aristocratic society of the period, and that dominance is felt in the works, often at times to an oppressive degree. One might even go so far as to say that the works from the *Kojiki* to the *Genji* are literary expressions of the process by which the Fujiwaras wrestled with their rivals and in time achieved a position of dictatorial control.

When we come to the *Konjaku*, however, we have a sense of newness and freedom, the freedom of a world that has at last been liberated from the weight of Fujiwara dominance.

NEMOTO: That is a very interesting way of looking at it.

IKEDA: Of course, the old Fujiwara-dominated world of the court aristocracy is undeniably reflected to some extent as well. There are even traces of a certain nostalgia for the traditional values, ideology, and culture of the preceding era, and a longing to return to them.

NEMOTO: Chapter twenty-two of the work contains biographies of members of the Fujiwara clan. And it has been surmised that chapter twenty-one, now lost, contained biographies of members of the imperial family.

IKEDA: The fact that such biographies were included in the work does not, I feel, spring from a sense of longing for the past. Rather, it reflects the fact that such material was necessary to the design of the work as a whole. If we turn to the fourth episode in chapter twenty-eight, which describes a *zuryō* (provincial governor), I think we can see what the writer's own position was. The passage describes a man who has been appointed governor of Owari and who proceeds happily to his new assignment: "The province was in a complete state of ruin, and the cultivation of the fields had utterly ceased. This governor was upright in heart and a man of excellent understanding and had governed wisely in the provinces that he had previously been assigned to. After arriving at his new assignment in Owari, he managed the affairs of government in a just manner, seeking only to enrich and benefit the region. Soon the peasants from neighboring provinces came flocking about in great numbers, leveling even the mountains and hills and opening up the land to cultivation. Thus, in the space of two years, the region became a model province."

In other words, he is pictured as a rare example of a wise and benevolent administrator, in contrast to the ordinary lot of governors of the time, who oppressed the peasants with a crushing burden of taxes.

NEMOTO: He is the exact opposite of the governor of Shinano, pictured in the thirty-eighth episode in the twenty-eighth chapter, who grabbed up all the land he could lay his hands on.

IKEDA: Yes. But later this same governor of Owari is ordered to take charge of the Gosechi dances and festivities at court. Because he is unfamiliar with the customs and etiquette of the court, he ends by being laughed at by the young courtiers of the upper rank. I do not necessarily feel that the author himself agreed with those who despised the governor. On the contrary, in his heart I think he sympathized with the governor and felt pity for him. And yet there is something in his attitude that suggests a kind of contempt for people with countrified manners.

NEMOTO: His attitude is a rather complex and subtle one. Though the identity of the author or the compiler of the *Konjaku* remains a mystery, it has been suggested that it may be the work of Minamoto no Takakuni (1004–77), who is popularly referred to as the Uji Dainagon. If so, then the work probably reflects the attitudes of the members of the upper aristocracy, among whom Minamoto no Takakuni would have been listed.

IKEDA: It has also been suggested that the author was a monk-scribe or a priest associated with some major temple. But I would like to consider this question of authorship at some future opportunity. Whoever the author may have been, I think the consciousness of the anomalies and contradictions of society that is reflected in the work does not represent the attitude or approach of any one individual. It is rather the manifestation of the particular kind of consciousness typical of an age of transition, when the old values and power structures are crumbling and the new powers that will take their place, the new values that will supplant them, have not yet assumed clear and definite form—in other words, an age of confusion.

A TRANSITIONAL WORK BETWEEN THE TALE OF GENJI AND THE TALE OF THE HEIKE

NEMOTO: The *Konjaku* was compiled at the time of the so-called *insei* system of government, when the retired emperors ruled from behind the scenes. For this reason it presents a very realistic picture of the period of transition from the court-centered government of the Heian period to the militaristic government of the period that followed. In the stories in chapter twenty-five in particular, which begin with the accounts of military rebels such as Taira no Masakado (d. 940) and Fujiwara no Sumitomo (d. 941), we have a very vivid depiction of the ideals and life styles of the new class of warrior leaders who were coming to prominence and who differed so markedly from the old aristocracy centered about the court.

IKEDA: The third episode, which deals with the battle between the two warriors Minamoto no Mitsuru and Taira no Yoshifumi, is particularly impressive. And the twelfth episode, which recounts how the famous Minamoto no Yorinobu (968–1048) and his son Yoriyoshi (998–1075) shot the horse thief, has a brisk and vigorous tone to it that departs completely from the air of stuffy elegance associated with the society of the Heian court. It is a special favorite of mine.

NEMOTO: Let us quote the scene of the encounter between the two warriors in the third episode: "They fixed their double-headed arrows to their bows and rode toward each other. First they allowed their arrows to fly at one another. With the second round of arrows, each one, determined this time to strike down his opponent without fail, drew his bow and let fly the arrow as he raced past his foe. When the two had passed one another, each wheeled his horse around, drew his bow, and this time, without discharging the arrow, swept past his opponent. Once more, when they had passed one another, they wheeled their horses about, drew their bows, and pressed them close to one another. Yoshifumi pressed forward with his bow and shot his arrow straight toward Mitsuru's body. Thereupon Mitsuru, making as though to drop from his horse, dodged the arrow, which struck the metal cover of his scabbard instead. Mitsuru then wheeled around and this time pressed his bow close to Yoshifumi's body, discharging his arrow. But Yoshifumi, dodging the arrow ——— his body, whereupon the arrow struck the plate of armor at the back of his waist."

As you can see, the passage employs a very simple style with many repetitions of phrases, and there are one or two words missing from the text. But it presents a clear and powerful description of the encounter between the two warriors. It is written in the style of language known as *Wa-Kan konkō*, which employs a mixture of native Japanese words and words and constructions borrowed from Chinese. It is wholly different from the more pure Japanese style used in the Heian-period tales and exercised a profound influence upon the military romances of the period that followed.

IKEDA: Not only in terms of style but in those of content as well, the *Konjaku* represents a transitional stage falling between the

Genji and the *Heike monogatari* (The Tale of the Heike), the great military epic of the Kamakura period (1185–1336). Its style is mixed, and its contents often contradictory in outlook, and yet it is a work that holds enormous fascination for the reader.

THE DISCOVERY OF ITS LITERARY VALUE

NEMOTO: For many centuries in the past, the *Konjaku* was utilized simply as a source for material on the period and was scarcely looked upon as a work of literature at all. Oddly enough, it was only when the twentieth-century fiction writer Ryūnosuke Akutagawa (1892–1927) began drawing upon it for the themes of many of his stories that its literary value came to be appreciated.

Akutagawa declared that the artistic worth and effectiveness of the *Konjaku* lay in its striking vividness. "And this vividness," he declared, "shines more barbarously than ever in the sections that deal with Japan. More barbarously than ever? Yes, I believe I have at last discovered the true nature of the *Konjaku monogatari*. . . . If I were to borrow a term from Western languages, I would describe it as the beauty of 'brutality'." [1]

IKEDA: Akutagawa's remarks on the *Konjaku* are very brief, and yet he defines the essence of the work with great clarity. As an example of the type of realistic description that gives the work its "vividness," he cites the story of the rabbit, the fox, and the monkey, the thirteenth episode in chapter five. In this story, a rabbit, a fox, and a monkey determine to practice the way of the Bodhisattva, devoting themselves unselfishly to the service of others. The god Indra, in order to test their resolve, changes himself into an old man and begs them to give him something to eat. The fox and the monkey immediately rush off and come back with various gifts of food. Thereupon: "The rabbit, encouraged to do likewise, took a torch, took up sticks of incense, and, curling back his tall ears, bulging out his eyes, drawing in his front paws, and opening wide his ass hole, walked east, west, north, and south searching, but he could not find anything at all."

In the end the rabbit builds a fire and, throwing himself into the flames, gives his own body as an offering to Indra. It is said that after his death he was reborn in the moon. The story is a famous one that most of us have heard from the time we were children.

The story is taken from such Chinese Buddhist works as the *Ta-T'ang hsi-yü-chi* (The Great T'ang Dynasty Record of Western Lands) and the *Fa-yüan chu-lin* (Dharma Gardens and Treasured Groves). But, as pointed out by Akutagawa, the Chinese versions of the story are much simpler. The passage of description in the *Konjaku* version that depicts the rabbit setting out on his search was apparently added by the *Konjaku* author. As Akutagawa remarks: "It is because this rabbit who lived so long ago in India is described with such vividness that we can clearly visualize him."

NEMOTO: The novelist Jirō Kojima (b. 1894) has also singled out this passage as an example of the "artless art" displayed in the writing of the *Konjaku*. The style is stumbling, juvenile, and wholly without literary artifice, and yet it succeeds in conveying a truly vivid picture of the rabbit.

WEALTH OF MATERIAL

IKEDA: Another thing that strikes one when reading the *Konjaku* is a new expansiveness, a turning outward toward the world at large in a way that was unknown in earlier Heian literature.

The *Genji* tends to focus itself upon the inner mental and spiritual life of the individual, and as a work of literature it is highly polished and elegant in form. By contrast the *Konjaku* confronts us with a tremendous wealth of materials and themes, but they are roughly hewn, often even crude in their presentation. The work gives an overall impression of incompleteness.

The fact that Akutagawa and other modern fiction writers have turned to it so often for themes is, in a sense, proof of both the richness of material it contains and the fact that such materials in the original are only imperfectly shaped and realized.

The world of the *Genji*, on the other hand, seems almost too narrow for such exploitation. Though there is a keen consciousness of the passing of time that underlies the novel, it is expressed in terms of a closed and rigidly confined environment. Occasionally we have glimpses of the common citizens of the capital and their lives, and now and then some character who is not a member of the court aristocracy will appear upon the scene. But the real interest of the author is never directed toward such persons or aspects of society. Her true concern is with the life of the upper classes. In this sense the *Genji* presents us with a segment of life deeply explored but narrow in its confines.

In comparison, the world of the *Konjaku* is shallower in presentation but vastly wider. Its cast of characters ranges from emperors and aristocrats to warriors, commoners, and even thieves and beggars. And whereas the *Genji* takes place almost entirely in the capital and its environs, the *Konjaku* ranges over the entire breadth of Japan.

NEMOTO: As scholars have pointed out, the only places in the whole of Japan as it existed at the time that are never mentioned in the *Konjaku* are the islands of Iki and Tsushima and the far western coastal area of Iwami. On the other hand, there is little attempt to portray the local characteristics of the numerous regions mentioned.

IKEDA: This last defect you mention is probably inevitable. After all, in those days it was impossible to travel in person to all the various regions mentioned and to get a sense of the local color, as a modern novelist writing about them would do.

And yet, the various tales and anecdotes recorded in the work must have been circulating about Japan over a considerable period of time, passing from the outlying regions to the capital, or from the capital to the outlying regions. What we have here is essentially a collection of bits of rumor and gossip that have been passed along from person to person and gradually shaped and expanded in the process. Since there were no media for rapid communication such as we are accustomed to today, such stories probably spread very slowly. And yet, as folklore studies have shown, though the rate of dissemination may have been very slow, such stories have an almost incredible capacity to make their way from one geographical area to another.

NEMOTO: Presumably there was some class in society that played a special role in the dissemination of such tales, a group comparable perhaps to the troubadours in European literature.

IKEDA: I think, as the poet and folklorist Shinobu Orikuchi (1887–1953) has suggested, that the shōdōshi had an important influence. The shōdōshi were men who endeavored to spread the Buddhist teachings abroad, among the populace as a whole. If the doctrines of Buddhism were to reach beyond the confines of the temples and monasteries, it is clear that some kind of effort must be made to explain and propagate them among the common people. Lofty and difficult disquisitions on the doctrines and philosophical principles of Buddhism were of no use for this. What was necessary were stories that would make Buddhism meaningful in terms of the daily lives of the populace. Such stories were no doubt cast in very different language from the discourses on the sutras delivered within the confines of the temples. They employed simple, everyday speech and were designed to arouse the interest of the listeners.

NEMOTO: There is no doubt that an enormous amount of

thought and effort went into the process of explaining the teachings of Buddhism in such a way that they would appeal to the hearts of the illiterate masses.

THE APPEARANCE OF A BODY OF POPULAR TALES

IKEDA: Hui-chiao, a Chinese monk of the Liang dynasty (502–56), wrote a work called the *Ch'ang-tao-lun* in which he discusses the principles of preaching to the populace. It is cited by Professor Yoshinori Nagai in his book entitled *Nihon Bukkyō bungaku* (Buddhist Literature in Japan). According to Hui-chiao, the preaching and propagation of the doctrine is not a matter of technical skill but depends rather upon the inner spirit of altruism that guides the person doing the preaching. At the same time, the essay gives an interesting picture of the ways in which the actual preaching should be carried out. It defines four elements that are vital to effective preaching—namely, voice, eloquence, talent, and breadth of learning. Thus we read: "If one lacks a proper voice, he will be unable to move his listeners. If he lacks eloquence, he will not be able to adapt his remarks to the particular occasion. If he lacks talent, then there will be no worthwhile content to his remarks. And if he lacks breadth of learning, then he will be unable to support his arguments." [2]

Hui-chiao also emphasizes that the content of one's preaching should be adapted to the particular type of person one is addressing. Professor Nagai sums up the rules for this as follows: (1) if one is addressing the five types of monks or nuns, one should speak eloquently on the impermanence of life and place great emphasis upon penitence; (2) if one is addressing rulers or other important persons of the aristocratic class, one should quote from secular literature and take care to speak in very refined language; (3) if one is addressing the commoners and the populace in general, one should speak in a concrete and realistic manner and explain the Truth in terms of actual experience; (4)

if one is addressing country people who are ignorant and uneducated, one should use homey language as a means to censure evil and encourage good.

NEMOTO: It sounds like very pertinent advice.

IKEDA: Of course, there were no doubt times when the person doing the preaching, in his eagerness to attract the attention of his listeners, adapted his message a little too freely to the tastes of the crowd and lost sight of his original objective. And at other times such persons must have used their skills simply as a means of earning a living. And yet, from what we have seen, it is not difficult to imagine how the themes and techniques that we read in later collections of popular tales could have grown up from the actual sermons and storytelling sessions of the shōdōshi preachers.

NEMOTO: The prototype of the *Konjaku* is said to be the *Nihonkoku gempō zennaku ryōiki* (Miraculous Stories of Karmic Retribution of Good and Evil in the Land of Japan), a collection of 116 Buddhist tales written in Chinese by a monk named Kyōkai from the Yakushi-ji temple in Nara. Though little is known about Kyōkai, he was probably originally a privately ordained monk who devoted himself to propagating Buddhism among the populace. The book was apparently completed around 823.

IKEDA: There seem to have been many such preachers of Buddhism among the common people of the time. During the Heian period, we hear of persons known as *hijiri* or *shami*, Buddhist monks or devotees who left the capital and journeyed about among the provinces, living as itinerant beggars and entertaining the populace with Buddhist tales as well as tales of a purely secular nature.

Such preaching monks were apparently accorded a very low position in the society of the time, and, in fact, many of them may have fallen into evil ways of life that were completely at variance with their religious vows. Thus, for example, the ninth episode in the twenty-ninth chapter of the *Konjaku* shows a certain Amida Hijiri who murders and then steals the luggage of a traveling companion who has just shared his noon meal with the culprit.

It was a transitional age, as we have seen, and one no doubt marked by many symptoms of social and moral confusion. And yet the origin of such itinerant preachers and their stock of tales is to be found, I believe, in a feeling of dissatisfaction with the established Buddhism of the time, which was centered about the great temples and monasteries, adapted to the tastes of the aristocracy, and hence wholly isolated from the lives of the common people.

NEMOTO: There are points in common with the social confusion experienced in Japan immediately after the end of the Pacific War or the situation we face today.

IKEDA: To turn back to the *Konjaku,* we notice that tales of evil and violence such as the one I have just referred to are wholly unknown in the literature of the Heian court aristocracy. Akutagawa has used two such anecdotes as the basis for his stories, the eighteenth episode in chapter twenty-nine, which is the source for his famous story "Rashōmon," and the twenty-third episode in the same chapter, which he has reworked in the story entitled "In a Grove." Such anecdotes reveal that there were thieves and rapists living almost under the noses of the elegant and refined aristocrats of the court. Reading these stories, it is difficult to imagine that they take place practically at the same time as the *Genji.* The first of these gives the following description of the great Rashōmon, the gate that stood at the southern entrance in the Heian capital: "In its upper story there were numerous bodies of dead persons. People who had no one to give them a proper burial were brought to the upper part of the gate and abandoned there."

NEMOTO: It is obvious that the social unrest and confusion and

the decay of orderly government had reached drastic pro-
portions. The fifteenth episode in the twenty-ninth chapter of
the *Konjaku* tells how the *kebiishi*, the capital police who were
supposed to prevent crime and preserve order, were caught
embezzling a large quantity of silk thread.

THE HUMAN COMEDY OF THE HEIAN PERIOD

IKEDA: Akutagawa expressed the greatest interest in the Japanese episodes of the *Konjaku*, particularly those dealing with
crimes or popular tales, the parts of the work that, as he put it,
"most closely resemble the human-interest stories in the daily
newspaper." Reading these sections, we can indeed see a new
age and world taking shape before our eyes. One other characteristic of the *Konjaku* is the fact that it presents us with a new
type of human being.

NEMOTO: Akutagawa has called it the *Human Comedy* of the
Heian period.

IKEDA: We have already noted that the work is unusual for the
variety of characters who appear and the fact that they represent all classes of society. It is also unique in the thoroughly
realistic manner in which it depicts human nature. Whereas
Lady Murasaki's characters are to some extent veiled in their
own beauty and we perceive them only indirectly, those of the
Konjaku are thrust before our eyes clearly and unabashedly, with
all the instincts, desires, and contentions that are basic to human
existence.

The quality that strikes one as foremost is the author's almost
insatiable curiosity with regard to human beings. He appears to
be interested in everything that pertains to men and women,
whether it reflects their good or their evil aspects.

His eyes seem to be drawn in particular to the darker side of
human nature, and this leads him at times into tales involving

violence and supernatural powers, stories of apparitions and ghostly transformations. There is a kind of earthy humor to his work that recalls the *Decameron* and other literary products of the Renaissance in Europe, and at the same time a strong suggestion of fin-de-siècle decadence.

NEMOTO: The question, of course, is what element it is in this collection of tales that makes it revelatory not only of a new age but of a new world and a new type of human being. The historian Shō Ishimoda, in his very suggestive work *Chūsei-teki sekai no keisei* (The Formation of the Medieval World), writes: "For earlier writers of literature in the *monogatari* (romance) form, there was no reality outside the society of the aristocrats and the capital. And because they were powerless to transcend these limitations, they were unable to discover any basic new entity or point of view that would permit them to reassess their conception of reality. As a result, their literature reached its highest point with the *Genji* and the *Utsubo monogatari,* and thereafter followed an inevitable course of decline. But these works represent only one aspect of Heian literature. It is important to note that there was a second and very significant aspect that was also taking shape. This is represented by such works as the *Shōmonki* (the earliest of the war tales), the *Michinoku waki,* and the *Konjaku.* The authorship of all these works is uncertain. The most important thing to note is that all represent the appearance of writers who had an interest in the new warrior society that was growing up in the provinces as an offshoot of the older aristocratic class. In other words, they discovered the existence of a separate world outside that of the old aristocratic society centered about the capital."[4]

I have quoted at considerable length, but I think it is interesting to note that Professor Ishimoda, examining the situation from the historical and sociological point of view, views the *Konjaku* as a kind of work of "self-criticism that grew up within the declining aristocratic society of the period."

THE PREJUDICED VIEW OF MODERN READERS

IKEDA: That is a very perceptive analysis, and I have no doubt that that aspect of the work represents an important innovation. But I would like to go a step farther and try to define a way in which it is more fundamentally innovative. If we do not do so, then I believe we can never fully comprehend the expansive world of the *Konjaku* in its full breadth.

What I am saying is that the world of the *Konjaku* is not made up simply of the type of "human interest" stories that Akutagawa admired. Nor is it entirely made up of stories that concern the new warrior class that was coming to the fore. Had these alone been the focus of interest, I hardly think they would have possibly provided a sufficient and clearcut motive for the gathering and recording of such an extensive and varied collection of tales.

There is a tendency among modern readers—Akutagawa is an example—to view the secular tales in the Japanese section of the *Konjaku* as constituting the genuinely worthwhile part of the book and to ignore the sections dealing with India and China and the Buddhist tales in the Japanese section. This, if I may speak very bluntly, represents, in my opinion, a highly prejudiced reading of the work.

NEMOTO: There is certainly that tendency. There are even editions of the *Konjaku* on the market now that simply omit the Buddhist tales entirely.

IKEDA: Perhaps in a sense such a view is inevitable, since, on the surface at least, the secular tales are often the most interesting. But we can hardly hope to arrive at a just appraisal of the *Konjaku* if we simply disregard the Buddhist tales, which easily comprise seven-tenths of the work as a whole.

NEMOTO: That is certainly an important point.

IKEDA: In the past the *Konjaku* was regarded as belonging to the category of Buddhist literature. As a result, ordinary readers tended to shy away from it. Apparently they felt that it was bound to be stuffy and sanctimonious.

In modern times, as interest has come to be focused on the secular tales, there has been a new appreciation of the literary value of the work, and it has also been reappraised in terms of its historical and sociological interest. These attempts to reevaluate the work represent important accomplishments. But they reflect an excessively modern interpretation that in the end has given us a distorted view of the classic as a whole.

NEMOTO: In other words, you believe that no attempt should be made to separate the Buddhist portions from the secular portions but that the work should be grasped in its entirety.

IKEDA: Exactly. At first glance, these two groups of material may appear to differ completely in conception and motivation. And yet I sense the same kind of extraordinary emotional excitement and commitment underlying them both. I cannot help feeling that both are pervaded by what I might call a kind of religious passion.

It was not mere creativity and the thirst for knowledge that led to the compilation of this vast and encyclopedic collection of tales. Rather, I feel that it is permeated with an almost obsessive passion to explore, through the act of compilation, the fundamental nature of the age and world in which the compiler or compilers lived, and of the men and women who peopled that world.

❖ ❖ ❖ ❖ ❖ ❖ ❖ ❖ ❖ ❖ ❖ ❖ ❖ ❖ ❖

8. Man as Seen in the Collections of Popular Tales

❖ ❖ ❖ ❖ ❖ ❖ ❖ ❖ ❖ ❖ ❖ ❖ ❖ ❖ ❖

BUDDHIST TALES AND SECULAR TALES

NEMOTO: It is customary to divide the contents of the *Konjaku* into two main categories: Buddhist tales and secular tales. Nowadays there is a tendency to regard the work as interesting and valuable mainly because of its secular tales, though the Buddhist tales clearly constitute the heart of the book.

IKEDA: I suppose we could say that that is correct. But if we stop to reconsider the matter, I wonder if we could not say that *all* the tales in the *Konjaku* are Buddhist.

NEMOTO: That is a very broad interpretation—certainly one that runs counter to the ordinary view.

IKEDA: Perhaps it does. But isn't that because there is a tendency to define the term "Buddhist tales" in too narrow a fashion? I do not see any reason why we must limit the category of Buddhist tales solely to those stories that deal overtly with Buddhist teachings or practices.

We have talked earlier concerning the numerous preachers who worked to spread a knowledge of Buddhism among the populace. When such men came to hold their storytelling sessions and expound the doctrine, we may be certain that they did not confine themselves to any single narrow category of tales such as are now labeled "Buddhist" but on the contrary attempted to work a large number of secular events and themes into their stories. Their aim was to make their stories as vivid and realistic as possible, so that they could create an impression of verisimilitude and literary excitement. At the end of the story, they customarily appended a moral, but this was little more than a mere convention. What was more important was the skill and realism with which the theme of the story itself was developed and handled.

NEMOTO: What you have just said might apply equally well to novels, plays, or even movies.

IKEDA: No matter how lofty the ideas an author or playwright may be trying to convey, if he does not have a sound and interesting story line, his work is almost certain to fall flat.

NEMOTO: But for the purposes of preaching Buddhist ideas to the population and giving concrete examples of their application, was it really necessary to have such a monstrous collection of tales as we find in the *Konjaku?*

IKEDA: No. If that had been the only aim of the stories, then something much simpler would have sufficed—a pamphlet or at most one of those slim paperbacks that are so popular these days. But in the *Konjaku* we clearly see a kind of richness and fertility of imagination that goes far beyond what would be needed to supply anecdotes and examples for the preacher. And in order to understand why this should be, we must try to understand the nature and thinking of the age in which the *Konjaku* was produced, to imagine for ourselves what it must have been like to live in such an age.

NEMOTO: You mean the consciousness of the fact that it was an age of transition?

IKEDA: The term "age of transition" has a very modern ring to it. If we try to use such concepts as an age of transition or a turning point in history to describe the period of the *Konjaku,* we may make it more understandable in terms of our contemporary ways of thought. But at the same time, if we are not careful, we may fail to perceive or appreciate the unique type of consciousness that prevailed in that period.

The age of the *Konjaku* was certainly, like our present age, one of transition, a turning point in history. But the people of the time never described it as such. They understood it rather in terms of *mappō* (the Latter Day of the Law), the concept of a final stage in the devolution of the Buddha's teachings, when evil was almost bound to prevail. That is the point I wish to make here.

NEMOTO: Their consciousness of the age was based upon Buddhist concepts of historical development.

IKEDA: Yes. And they were keenly conscious of the fact that the world was said to have entered the period of the Latter Day of the Law, conscious to a degree that it is perhaps difficult for those of us today to imagine. We can see it clearly reflected in the writings of the educated persons of the time.

"These days the monks of Mount Hiei are brawling, and those of the eastern and western pagodas engage in battle. Sometimes they set fire to and burn down each other's quarters, Sometimes they fall victim to each other's arrows. The cloisters for religious study and practice have on the contrary become the courts of war. Has the time already come when the Law of the Buddha will be wiped out and destroyed?" (*Chūyūki,* 1104)

"A wicked age with all the five pollutions, an age of contention and stubbornness: will such rebellion and lawlessness continue without end? It is pitiable, pitiable!" (*Gyokuyō*, 1185)

"Nowadays people all say that we have reached the age of the Middle and Latter Day of the Law. Disasters now will be our fate." (*Gonki*, 1000)

Reading such entries in the diaries of the time, we see that there was a widespread feeling that a time of crisis was at hand when the teachings of Shākyamuni Buddha would be wiped out.

NEMOTO: The writers seem to apprehend it not as a doctrinal concept, but as an actual experience in their lives.

Motives for the Compilation of the Konjaku Monogatari

IKEDA: According to the *Fusō ryakki*, a historical work compiled at the end of the Heian period, 1052 marked the beginning of the Latter Day of the Law, also known as the period of the degenerate Dharma. The *Konjaku* is thought to have been compiled around the beginning of the twelfth century, by which time the belief that the world had entered upon an era of degeneracy and religious decline must have been even more deeply felt.

In the *Nihon gempō zen'aku ryōiki*, compiled at the beginning of the ninth century and referred to earlier, we find, in the preface to the third chapter, a reference to the doctrine of the so-called three periods or ages: "If we study all the discourses Shākyamuni made during his lifetime, we learn that there are three periods: first, the period of the true Dharma [*shōbō*], which lasts five hundred years; second, the period of the counterfeit Dharma [*zōhō*], lasting a thousand years; and third, the period of the degenerate Dharma [mappō], which continues for ten thousand years. . . . How can we fail to be more careful? It is useless to repent after spending a lifetime in vain. Who can enjoy immortality since one is given a limited life? How can one depend on one's transient life as being eternal? We are already in the age of the degenerate Dharma. How can we live without doing good? My heart aches for all beings. How can we be saved from calamity in the age of the degenerate Dharma?"[1]

The author of this work clearly calculated the beginning of the mappō era in a different fashion from that adopted in the *Fusō ryakki,* since he believed that by his time the world had already entered the mappō era. It is obvious, however, that the belief in the period of the degenerate Dharma was already important as early as the ninth century.

Another important phrase at this time was *byakuhō ommotsu, tōjō gonshō* (the disappearance of the Great Law, strife and contention), which derives from the *Daishikkyō*. It indicates an age of turmoil when established religions, values, and systems of thought fall into decay.

NEMOTO: And you are suggesting that it was this consciousness of the age in which he was living that motivated the compiler of the *Konjaku* to undertake his work?

IKEDA: We do not know who the compiler may have been. But I have a feeling that, living in an age of chaos, he was filled with a fervent desire to strengthen the foundations of human existence, which seemed to have become so infirm, and to rebuild a world that had broken into pieces. I would like to see the *Konjaku* as a search for some new religion or system of thought that would bring that about. It is for this very reason that the compiler begins by turning his attention to India and the origins of the Buddhist religion and then proceeds to trace its growth and change through the later periods of history.

NEMOTO: Certainly that aim seems to be apparent in the conception of the work.

IKEDA: If we look at the specifically Buddhist tales in the work, we will see that nearly all of them are taken from earlier works, such as the *Kako genzai inga-kyō*, the *Butsuhon-gyōju-kyō*, or the *Hōon jurin*. The compiler of the *Konjaku* has copied out these stories with almost no change or elaboration, merely translating them from Chinese into Japanese. Thus these portions of his work may be said to be of interest simply as translations.

NEMOTO: Some critics have surmised that he must have found it a rather tiresome task, copying out stories from so many old texts.

IKEDA: That's a rather cynical view. Present-day readers may find little of interest in these sections of the work. But if we try to see them in a fresh light, I don't think we need find them dull at all. Even though the compiler was merely copying from earlier works, I believe that, as I said before, he felt himself to be engaged in a fundamental and vital undertaking, one that he gave himself to with great passion. He was clearly not among the creators of the new age—he was not a reformer or a man of action. And even though he was motivated by religious fervor, he was not a profound thinker or sage, not the kind who sets forth some grand and lofty system of thought. By temperament he was not suited for any of these occupations. His temperament was rather that of a compiler and an observer who devoted himself to these activities with extraordinary energy.

NEMOTO: And he happened to live just at a time when numerous changes were taking place.

IKEDA: Yes. The great system of Buddhist philosophy that was represented by the Tendai sect of Mount Hiei had reached the point where no new logical development was possible. At the same time, the monasteries of Mount Hiei themselves had fallen into a state of degeneracy, the monks giving themselves up to brawling and contention. What had been a living system of thought had devolved into an empty ideology, one whose end was already in sight.

On the other hand, though we may already see the stirrings of what eventually was to be a new religious movement, the time was not yet ripe for its appearance. The emergence of a great new Dharma, one that would put an end to the age of the Latter Day of the Law when the older Dharma had disappeared, was still to come.

The chaotic conditions that prevailed tended to lead men into discouragement and decadence. I believe, however, that although the compiler of the *Konjaku* must at times have felt himself about to be sucked down into the decadence of the age, he continued to work away at his labor of compilation as a means of resisting and struggling to overcome that fate. But perhaps I am indulging too much in mere speculation.

LEGENDARY ACCOUNTS OF SHĀKYAMUNI

NEMOTO: On the contrary. By doing so, you seem to make the unknown compiler of the work easier to imagine as a person.

IKEDA: The *Konjaku* opens with eight episodes that describe Shākyamuni, the founder of Buddhism, beginning with his conception and birth and tracing his career up to the time when he achieved Enlightenment. Personally, I find these tales extremely interesting. And at the same time, they serve strikingly to reveal the compiler's attitude regarding the figure of Shākyamuni.

NEMOTO: I think it would be well to quote the entire text of the first episode, which relates how the Buddha Shākyamuni appeared in the world of mankind.

"Long ago, before the Buddha Shākyamuni had attained Buddhahood, he was known as the Bodhisattva Shākyamuni and dwelt in a place called the Inner Court of the Tushita Heaven. When he made up his mind to be born into the land of Jambu-dvīpa [the world of mankind], he displayed the five signs of decay. The five signs of decay are these. First, though a celestial being does not blink, he began to blink. Second, though the flowers in the hair of a celestial being never fade, the flowers in his hair faded. Third, though the robes of a celestial being never become soiled with dirt and dust, his robes became soiled. Fourth, though a celestial being never sweats, the sweat began to pour from his armpits. Fifth, though a celestial being never changes his original status, he found that he could no longer remain in his original status.

"At this time, when the other celestial beings saw these signs appear in the Bodhisattva, they were puzzled and said to the Bodhisattva: 'Today, when we see these signs that you have manifested, we are disturbed and our minds are confused. We beg you to tell us the reason for them.'

"The Bodhisattva thereupon replied to the celestial beings, saying: 'You must understand that all phenomena that are conditioned are impermanent in nature. Now before long I shall leave this heavenly palace and be born in the land of Jambu-dvīpa.' When the celestial beings heard this, they lamented greatly. Then the Bodhisattva thought to himself, when I am born into the land of Jambu-dvīpa, who shall my father be and who shall my mother be? And he decided, it will be sufficient if I have as my father Shuddodana, the king of Kapilavastu, and as my mother Queen Māyā, his consort.

"In the year of the cyclical sign Mizu no to Ushi, the eighth day of the seventh month, he entered the womb of Queen Māyā. As Queen Māyā lay sleeping that night, she dreamed that the Bodhisattva came riding through the air on a white elephant with six tusks and entered her body through her right side. Her body became clear and transparent, as though an object were being placed inside a glass jar. The queen woke with a start and, hastening to the side of King Shuddodana, she told him of her dream. When the king heard the account of her dream, he said: 'I too have had the same dream. But I am not capable of divining what the dream means.' So saying, he hurriedly sent a summons to a brahman who was skilled at reading signs and, presenting him with wonderful gifts of fragrant flowers and various kinds of food and drink, he asked the meaning of the queen's dream. The brahman said to the king: 'The queen has conceived a royal son who has many good and wonderful signs about him. I cannot describe them all in detail. But for the sake of Your Majesty, I will describe them in brief. This son who is within the womb of the queen will surely be a glorious scion of the Shākya people. When he comes forth from the womb, he will emit a great brilliance. Brahmā, Indra, and the other celestial beings will all pay him honor. The signs are very auspicious and show that he will surely become a Buddha. And if he should remain within the household and not take up the religious life, he will become a great Wheel-turning King who will fill the four continents with all the seven precious things and will have a thousand sons.'

"At this time, when the king heard these words of the brahman, he was filled with a boundless joy, and he presented him with gold and silver and other treasures such as elephants, horses, and carriages. The queen also presented him with various treasures. The brahman accepted all the treasures that the king and queen gave to him and carried these away with him when he departed. Thus has it been related."

As this episode illustrates, the first chapter of the *Konjaku* presents a biography of Shākyamuni as he has traditionally been depicted in story and legend.

IKEDA: Yes. There are many elements in the stories indicating a process of deification. Such elements, though merely legend, were no doubt added out of a desire to pay honor to Shākyamuni's greatness. Certain of these elements, such as the five signs of decay of a celestial being, or the concepts of the

Buddha and the Chakravarti-rāja (Wheel-turning King), give us clues concerning the starting point of the Buddhist religion and the goals at which it aims. Like the legend of the Four Meetings, which tells how on various occasions the young Shākyamuni encountered an old man, a sick man, a corpse, and a religious man, and thereby determined to enter the religious life himself, they have a deep symbolic significance.

NEMOTO: Chapter five of the *Konjaku* also contains a number of *jātaka*—birth stories, or tales of the Buddha in his previous incarnations—that are of great interest from a literary point of view.

IKEDA: This chapter includes the story of the rabbit, the fox, and the monkey (episode thirteen), which we have already talked about, as well as such other tales as that of the nine-colored deer (eighteen), the fox and the lion (twenty), the fox that borrowed the might of the tiger (twenty-one), and the turtle that received the liver of a living monkey (twenty-five)—moralistic fables that remind one of Aesop.

NEMOTO: Chapters six to ten deal with China. The tenth contains stories taken from Chinese history and would appear to have the least direct connection with Buddhism itself.

IKEDA: Yes. Strictly speaking, these are not Buddhist tales at all. And yet some of them, such as that dealing with the "three joys" of the philosopher Yung Ch'i-chi'i (episode ten), Li Kuang's piercing of a stone with an arrow (seventeen), or the jade of Pien Ho (twenty-nine), are referred to in the *Gosho* of Nichiren Daishōnin. He no doubt took them directly from works of Chinese history and philosophy rather than from the *Konjaku*. But they prove that even secular tales and anecdotes can be used to illustrate points of Buddhist doctrine.

NEMOTO: The section of the work dealing with Japanese Buddhism begins with chapter eleven. Thus the work traces the history of Buddhism from its origin in India to its eventual introduction and growth in Japan. In a sense, therefore, the *Konjaku* probably represented the most comprehensive history of Buddhism, or collection of materials on the history of Buddhism, in existence in Japan at the time.

A Growing Consciousness of the World at Large

IKEDA: Probably so. The actual tales collected in the work are in some ways very uneven in quality and interest. And yet one must surely praise the high intentions of the compiler.

NEMOTO: We can see that the compiler was not motivated simply by nostalgia for the past or antiquarianism in his efforts to gather together a systematic compilation of records or historical materials. His historical consciousness is founded upon an intense concern for the age in which he himself was living and a desire to understand its problems.

IKEDA: And I would like to stress that he manifests not only a consciousness of history, of the development of events in time, but also a consciousness of the world at large, of the spatial as well as the temporal dimension.

In the episode we have quoted above, we encountered the term Embudai, the land of Jambu-dvīpa. In meaning, it is equivalent to what we would call "the world" as a whole. The *Konjaku* displays an interest in this broader concept of the world to a degree that is probably unparalleled among the classics of Japanese literature.

NEMOTO: For the Japanese of the time, Embudai meant India, China, and Japan; in this sense the *Konjaku* does deal with the entire known world of the time.

IKEDA: And in doing so, it reflects the universal nature of the Buddhist religion, a world religion that transcends the boundaries of race and nationality. This, I believe, is the reason why a work such as the *Konjaku,* though produced in an age when Japan was relatively cut off from the outside world, still displays this kind of broad consciousness of the world as a whole.

Of course, we can hardly say that this world consciousness is based upon any systematic grasp of the world as a whole or knowledge of its actual structure. Nor does it manifest the kind of positive awareness of the community of mankind that we are accustomed to today. In actual fact, no such awareness of the world as a whole had come into being anywhere at the time.

The world in the *Konjaku* is conceived as a flat area, its regions to be merely enumerated in the order in which they appear. Nor is it something to be actively explored; it is mere circumstance that brings it within one's line of vision.

I therefore do not wish to appear to be praising this aspect of the *Konjaku* too extravagantly. And yet the fact that the compiler, in the first episode of the fifth chapter, takes care to relate the legend of the founding of the far-off kingdom of Ceylon, or tells us of the customs of the "Country Where They Cast Away the Aged," indicates that he had a genuine if rather naive interest in the world at large. Though it may have been inspired by a superficial taste for the exotic, his determination to fix his eyes upon the regions far beyond the sea is something that cannot be lightly dismissed.

NEMOTO: It differs, then, from the present-day passion for travel abroad, which is a result of the leisure and affluence of modern life.

IKEDA: It differs from the present day precisely because the compiler lived in a closed society, at a time when Japan was cut off from the rest of the world and foreign travel was all but unknown.

NEMOTO: The compiler more closely resembles the intellectuals of Japan in the late Tokugawa period, who also were intensely interested in learning about the world outside Japan.

IKEDA: I'm not sure that comparison is very accurate. The compiler of the *Konjaku* was, after all, concerned with reflections upon the history of the past, not with the immediate present or future of the world.

NEMOTO: This may be changing the subject somewhat, but the thirty-second episode of chapter ten tells a story of how two thieves, father and son, broke into a king's storehouse and stole his treasures, after which the son killed the father. Though the setting is China, Minoru Kida has pointed out that it bears a striking resemblance to a story told by the Greek historian Herodotus in his *Histories*. [2]

Chinese works such as the *Fa-yüan chu-lin* have been shown to be the source of most of the *Konjaku's* tales. But such similarities in theme and characters point to certain universal traits that are shared in common by the tales of China, India, Egypt, and Greece.

IKEDA: That is a very interesting observation.

NEMOTO: In our earlier discussion of the *Kojiki*, we stressed the widespread nature of certain myths or themes in mythology. If the same is true in the case of the *Konjaku* stories, we can only be amazed at the power of such tales to spread from one culture to another.

KEEN OBSERVATION OF REALITY

IKEDA: The awareness of time and the world at large that we see in the *Konjaku* is firmly rooted in reality. Or, to put it another way, such an awareness could not help but result in a keen observation of the real world.

We have already talked about the new view of humanity that emerges in the Japan sections of the *Konjaku*. Part of this new view is manifested in an interest in various occupations and classes of society or the life and customs of the provincial areas of Japan, interests that are scarcely reflected at all in earlier works of Heian literature such as the *Genji*.

NEMOTO: Anecdotes such as the twenty-seventh and twenty-eighth of chapter fifteen, which deal with *etori bōshi,* or priests of the outcast class, or the stories dealing with sumo wrestlers in chapter twenty-three, are particularly unusual and provide valuable insights into the customs and society of the time.

IKEDA: But these, of course, display a mere surface novelty, a novelty confined to the subject matter. The truly striking thing about the *Konjaku's* image of human beings lies, as I have stressed earlier, in the manner in which they are perceived and depicted. For example, the eighteenth episode in chapter twenty-eight, which describes quarrels between monks, exposes in merciless fashion the ugly desires that lie within the hearts of the monks themselves. And the stories that Akutagawa has utilized in his "The Nose" and "Yam Gruel" (chapter twenty-eight, episode twenty, and chapter twenty-six, episode seventeen) present remarkably explicit depictions of the pettiness and folly of human vanity.

At the same time, there are others that give powerful affirmation of the dignity of human life and the kind of bravery that defies the superstitions of the times. An example is the seventh episode in chapter twenty-six, which depicts the grief of the parents of a young girl who has been chosen to be a living sacrifice to the fearful monkey god. In this episode, the "man from the east" addresses the parents in these words: "For men in this world, there is nothing more important than life itself. And of all men's treasures, there is none more precious than children. And yet you see your only daughter about to be chopped up into mincemeat before your eyes, and you remain helpless and ineffectual. . . . When it is a matter of life or death, even the Buddhas and gods may do fearful things; even for the sake of one's own child, a person may hesitate to put his life in danger."

NEMOTO: The writer seems determined to depict human instincts and desires just as they are, without any idealization.

IKEDA: Exactly.

NEMOTO: Some would view this attitude of the writer to be in a sense irreligious or even antireligious. In other words, though the *Konjaku* may have been conceived originally as a collection of Buddhist tales, there would appear to be many elements in it that belie its constant exhortations to "have faith in the Three Treasures."

One wonders if the compiler of the *Konjaku* did not deviate along the way from his original purpose. And it is precisely in those places where he deviated from it that we discover his new view of the human being and encounter the passages of his work that are of greatest value as literature.

IKEDA: That is a suspicion that it is hard to deny. As a matter of fact, there are rather a large number of tales that, in the name of religious concern, appear to be drawn much too far in the direction of violence and a taste for the bizarre. And yet it is precisely in such tales, I believe, that we see the peculiar nature of the religious consciousness characteristic of this age of crisis that the men of the time called the Latter Day of the Law.

For instance, chapters eleven to twenty, which deal with Buddhism in Japan, are arranged so as to constitute a kind of biographical survey of Japanese Buddhism from the time of its inception to the period of the writer. And yet within these chapters we can already see signs of the decay of the older established religious organizations and powers.

NEMOTO: The main focus of attention is upon reverence for the *Lotus Sutra*. But particularly striking are the stories that deal with the miraculous powers of the Bodhisattvas Kannon and Jizō and those dealing with rebirth in the Pure Land.

Among the stories dealing with the miraculous powers of Kannon, there are some, such as the twenty-eighth episode in chapter sixteen, on the Warashibe Chōja, a man who built up a fortune out of nothing but rice stalks; these kinds of stories contain elements that are very questionable from a religious point of view. And then we have the man in the fourteenth episode of the same chapter who manifested his devotion to Kannon by praying each day: "Homage to Kannon! Please give me ten thousand *kan* of copper coins, ten thousand *koku* of white rice, and many beautiful girls."*

IKEDA: On the other hand, in the stories in chapter nineteen concerning the causes that led various persons to enter the religious life, we find the hardships of human life depicted with great vividness. These are people who, as Akutagawa puts it, "groan with the miseries of the temporal world." Akutagawa himself has quoted the story of how Ōmi no Sadamoto came to enter the priesthood (second episode). These and many of the other episodes like it present very striking depictions of the sufferings of birth, old age, sickness, and death and the sadness of parting from loved ones.

NEMOTO: In the episodes in chapter fifteen dealing with famous monks, those concerning Zōga and Genshin are particularly impressive, depicting religious men who are quite different from those associated with the older Buddhism of the aristocracy.

A RELIGIOUS MONUMENT

IKEDA: Reading these various sections of the work, we get a very clear and realistic picture of the common people of the day, living in a period believed to be that of the Latter Day of the Law, constantly harrassed by trouble and sorrow, and in many cases turning to religion only in the hope of gaining some worldly benefit.

*One *kan* equals 3.75 kilograms; one *koku* equals 180 liters.

In the eyes of the compiler of the *Konjaku,* the reality of the world was no doubt apprehended as a manifestation of the constant transmigration of beings in the six realms of existence. As Akutagawa declares: "The realms of ashura demons, hungry spirits, hell, or animals do not exist anywhere other than in the present world." And the realm of the four evil inclinations— those toward anger, greed, ignorance, sycophancy, and similar passions—is in the end none other than the present world. These exist within the makeup of each individual. This, I believe, was the image of human beings that the compiler of the *Konjaku* had in mind, one that he perceived not as a concept but as a fact of actual experience.

NEMOTO: Yes, that certainly describes the secular world, the world of evil deeds, as it is depicted in the *Konjaku.* But among the categories of the ten states of existence, the six realms constitute only the six lower states of existence. Above them are the four noble states—those of the Buddha, the Bodhisattva, the *shōmon* (shrāvaka), and the *engaku* (pratyeka-buddha). I would like to think that these higher states of existence are described in the specifically Buddhist sections of the work.

IKEDA: I believe they are. In fact, I would like to speculate that the compiler of the *Konjaku* was trying to construct his work in such a way that it would function as a chart or illustration of all the ten states of existence.

NEMOTO: But in the concept of the ten states, a certain con- sciousness of values is needed in order to move from the six lower states or realms to the four higher ones. This point does not seem to come across very clearly in the *Konjaku.* Or rather, to put it another way, the compiler of the *Konjaku* seems to be more concerned with the drama played out in the six lower states and to respond more sympathetically to its inhabitants than he does to those of the higher states.

IKEDA: Yes. This reflects, I think, the literary temperament of the compiler of the *Konjaku*. And at the same time, it probably represents the actual reality of the Latter Day of the Law, when established values and standards no longer exercised the authority they once had. Confronted with this reality, the compiler, rather than seeking to judge his material or impose a moral order upon it, chose to toss it all into the crucible of his work, with all its inherent chaos and contradictions just as they were. No doubt he was unable to foresee clearly just what would emerge from the crucible. At all times he maintains the attitude of a moral relativist, observing reality and mankind through the eyes of chaos.

NEMOTO: Such a view helps one better to understand the atmosphere of moral chaos that characterizes the work as a whole.

IKEDA: On the surface, at least, the emphasis seems to be less upon the move upward from the six lower states to the four noble states of the higher level than it is upon the opposite process, and this probably reflects the compiler's own approach. But I would like to think that, if we consider the matter more deeply, this is an indication of the basic nature of Buddhism and the point of departure of the Buddhist religion.

I feel strongly that the first episode in the book has a very deep and vital bearing upon this point. We have already quoted the episode in full above. And as we saw at that time, the Bodhisattva Shākyamuni, who was dwelling in the "Inner Court of the Tushita Heaven," abandoned his heavenly palace and descended to earth to be born in the land of Jambu-dvīpa. And later, he abandoned the glory and ease of his position as heir apparent to Shuddhodana and entered the religious life. The anecdote of the Four Meetings presents in symbolic form the reasons that impelled him to take this step.

NEMOTO: He determined to find a solution to the problems of

birth, sickness, old age, and death—to the basic ills of human existence.

IKEDA: To some extent, of course, the compiler of the *Konjaku* views man as trapped within the six realms or lower states of existence, destined to transmigrate endlessly from one to another without ever escaping. But if I were to speculate upon what went on within his mind, I would say that he had a certain premonition of events to come. I say this because, although the age of the Latter Day of the Law represents a critical time of transition, the end of a long era of degeneration, it at the same time announces the coming of a new era in the future.

It is always darkest just before dawn, the proverb tells us. Thus this midnight period, which spelled the extinction of the Dharma, held within it the promise of an epochal new religious reformation and renaissance.

The compiler of the *Konjaku* clearly stopped just one step short of that new era. In the chaos of the period in which he lived, he could not tell what was to come. And yet I believe that in his heart he undoubtedly perceived with great certainty that such a new era was drawing near and, in fact, could not help but arrive in time.

Perhaps once more I am allowing myself to be carried away by emotional speculation. And yet if we would understand the *Konjaku* not in terms of its various parts but as a total work of literature, we can do no better than to view it as in a sense a religious monument erected in a time of unprecedented crisis.

Notes

Chapter 1

[1]Takashi Inukai, *Man'yō no tabi* [Man'yoshu Journeys] (Tokyo, 1974), preface.

[2]This translation, slightly modified, is taken from the Nippon Gakujutsu Shinkōkai translation of one thousand poems, *The Man'yōshū* (New York, 1965), p. 3.

[3]*Ibid.*, p. 181.

[4]*Ibid.*, p. 293.

[5]*Ibid.*, p. 179.

[6]*Ibid.*, p. 200.

[7]*Ibid.*, p. 207

[8]*Ibid.*, p. 50

[9]*Ibid.*, p. 192.

Chapter 2

[1]Nippon Gakujutsu Shinkōkai, *Man'yōshū*, pp. 212–13.

[2]Donald L. Philippi, trans., *Kojiki* (Princeton and Tokyo, 1969), p.

248. The spelling of the place name Heguri has been changed to conform with modern pronunciation.

[3]*Ibid.*, p. 176.
[4]*Ibid.*, p. 41
[5]*Ibid.*, p. 271.
[6]*Ibid.*, p. 66.
[7]*Ibid.*, p. 72.
[8]*Ibid.*, p. 47.
[9]*Ibid.*, p. 232.
[10]*Ibid.*, p. 248.

Chapter 3

[1]Philippi, *Kojiki*, p. 53.
[2]Emperor Kōtoku, fifth year of Hakuchi. Cf. W. G. Aston, *Nihongi* (Tokyo and Rutland, 1972 reprint), p. 246.
[3]Philippi, *Kojiki*, p. 85.
[4]*Ibid.*, p. 129–30.

Chapter 4

[1]The translation is that by Edward G. Seidensticker, *The Tale of Genji* (New York, 1976), p. 409.
[2]*Ibid.*, p. 345.
[3]Nippon Gakujutsu Shinkōkai, *Man'yōshū*, p. 11.
[4]Seidensticker, *Genji*, p. 357.
[5]*Ibid.*, p. 699.
[6]Edward Seidensticker, *The Gossamer Years* (New York and Rutland, 1964), p. 69.
[7]Ivan Morris, *As I Crossed a Bridge of Dreams* (New York, 1971), p. 122.

Chapter 5

[1]Seidensticker, *Genji*, p. 790.
[2]*Ibid.*, p. 437.
[3]*Ibid.*, p. 640.
[4]*Ibid.*, p. 734.

[5]*Ibid.*, p. 634.
[6]*Ibid.*, p. 737.
[7]Philip Wayne, trans., *Faust, Part One* (Middlesex, England, 1949),
p. 44.

Chapter 6

[1]Seidensticker, *Genji*, p. 339.
[2]*Ibid.*, p. 91.
[3]*Ibid.*, p. 869.
[4]*Ibid.*, pp. 1071–72.
[5]*Ibid.*, pp. 437–38.
[6]*Ibid.*, p. 720.
[7]*Ibid.*, p. 724.
[8]*Ibid.*, p. 867.
[9]*Ibid.*, p. 1018.
[10]*Ibid.*, p. 733.
[11]*Ibid.*, p. 1089.

Chapter 7

[1]Ryūnosuke Akutagawa, *"Konjaku monogatari ni tsuite"* [On the *Tales of Once Upon a Time*], an essay included in the complete works of Ryūnosuke Akutagawa.
[2]Quoted in Yoshinori Nagai, *Nihon Bukkyō bungaku* [Buddhist Literature in Japan] (Tokyo, 1963), pp. 175–6.
[3]Shō Ishimoda, *Chūsei-teki sekai no keisei* [The Making of Japan's Medieval World] (Tokyo, 1957), p. 240.

Chapter 8

[1]Kyoko Motomochi Nakamura, trans., *Miraculous Stories from the Japanese Buddhist Tradition* (Cambridge, Mass., 1973), p. 221–22. The translation has been slightly modified.
[2]*Histories*, vol. 2, section 121.

Glossary-Index

aesthetic sensibility of Japanese, 64–67

Aikoku hyakunin isshu (One Hundred Poems of One Hundred Patriots), 40

Akutagawa, Ryūnosuke, novelist, 64, 162, 163, 164, 168, 169, 186, 188, 189

Amaterasu Ōmikami, sun goddess, 52, 62, 63, 68, 83, 90

Amidist Buddhism, 138, 139, 140, 141

Aston, W. G., 17

Azuma uta, see "Eastland Poems"

Benten (Benzaiten), Japanese deity, 77

Book of Odes, 25

Buddhism, 40–44, 73, 77–91, 109, 121–32, 135–52, 172–83, 186–91; reflected in *Man'yōshū,* 40–44; reflected in *Kojiki,* 73, 77, 80–92; influence and concepts of in *Genji monogatari,* 109, 121–32, 135–52; reflected in *Konjaku monogatari,* 172–83, 186–91

Buddhist tales in *Konjaku monogatari,* 174–79

chōka: "long poem," 15

Chronicles of Japan, see Nihon shoki

civilization versus nature, 100–103

classics, defined, 9–10; appreciation of, 10–11

Collection of Ten Thousand Poems, see Man'yōshū

The "weathermark" identifies this book as a production of John Weatherhill, Inc., publishers of fine books on Asia and the Pacific. Supervising editor: James T. Conte. Book design and typography: Miriam F. Yamaguchi. Production supervisor: Mitsuo Okado. Composition and printing, in offset: Komiyama Printing Company, Tokyo. Binding: Makoto Binderies, Tokyo. The typeface used is 12-point Monophoto Baskerville.